HAUNTED JOLIET PRISON

WENDY MOXLEY ROE

Haunted
America

Published by Haunted America
A Division of The History Press
Charleston, SC
www.historypress.com

First published 2020

Manufactured in the United States

ISBN 9781467147163

Library of Congress Control Number: 2020941938

For my mom and dad, who passed down to me their love of spooky movies, history and local ghost lore.

For the loves of my life, Erin, Sam, Tucker and Sylar, anything is possible.

Photograph by Karl K.

"When I came back from Joliet,
There was a new courthouse with a dome.
For I was punished like all who destroy
The past for the sake of the future."

—*Edgar Lee Masters, "Silas Dement,"* Spoon River Anthology

CONTENTS

PREFACE

M y experience with haunted places began in the fall of 2012, when I walked into Bachelor's Grove Cemetery in Midlothian, Illinois. What I felt that day was life changing. It opened a path for me that I would never have thought possible ten years ago.

I have always said that Bachelor's Grove came to me, not the other way around. I truly believe that when you open yourself to the possibilities, what is meant to be will naturally find you. My work with Bachelor's Grove is what led me to the Old Joliet Prison. The prison, like Bachelor's Grove, seemed to fall into my lap—or more precisely, into my head and heart.

One bright, sunny day in May of 2014, I took a drive with my friend Karl to the Joliet Iron Works Park to meet a group for a ghost box session investigation. I am originally from the Baltimore area and moved to Chicago in 2008, so at that point, I had only been to Joliet once a few years before and knew very little about the area. As is normal for me, I soon wandered away from the group to explore with my camera in hand. I walked to the very back of the park, where the path becomes more isolated in a long row of trees that are dotted by electric towers on either side. I had seen train tracks earlier and knew the trees to my right could not be as thick as they seemed. A short way ahead, a footpath appeared in the trees on my right, confirming my suspicions. My natural curiosity led me along that path, where I hoped to find and photograph more of the abandoned warehouses I had seen earlier.

With my eyes firmly on the ground in front of me, I finally emerged on the other side of the trees and immediately saw the train tracks a few feet

Old Joliet Prison as it looks today, in 2020. *Author's collection.*

away. The first thing I noticed was an old shed-type building on the other side of the tracks. There was a fence around it, but I wondered why there was razor wire on top. As I looked up, I saw, for the first time, one of the large and menacing guard towers of Old Joliet Prison—although, at the time, I did not know what it was. I cannot properly describe in words my first impression. It is imprinted in me. That first-glimpse snapshot in my brain was accompanied by a feeling akin to being punched in the gut. I felt dread, sadness, excitement, despair, horror, life and death all swirling together. That feeling is seared brilliantly clear into my memory. I remember thinking, "What the hell is that?" I knew from that moment that this place was *significant.*

When I gathered my senses, I crossed the tracks to get a closer look and noticed that there was an opening in the fence. I contemplated going through, but my gut said that finding Karl first would be the safest thing, as no one knew where I was. Just as that very creepy thought flashed in my head, Karl popped out of the opening in the gate, scaring the bejesus out of me. I should have known he was one step ahead of me.

We explored an outer building, which I later identified as the receiving building, at the back of the property and eventually walked back to meet up with some of the others from our original group. After explaining what

Train tracks behind the prison and South Wall. *Author's collection.*

we had found, several of us decided to explore a little farther. Following a beaten path through a couple of fences, we ended up on the front steps of Old Joliet Prison. To our surprise, the front doors were open. As we all cautiously went through the entrance, we took in every bit of the place. Some of the group's members noticed that the iron-barred gates that lead to the actual prison cells were also open. Those few, including Karl, took off into the dark beyond those iron doors. The others and I carefully explored the entrance. I was scared to death; something in me knew that this was too good to be true and was aware of the dangers of being in the old, unkempt building.

My group finally decided to venture through the big iron gates, too, but just as we went to pass through them, two Illinois Department of Corrections (IDOC) officers carrying very large pump shotguns came through from the other side. I spun so fast in the opposite direction that I'm surprised I did not fall. They asked what we were doing there, and we replied that we were tourists taking photos. They responded, "How did you get in?" We said, "Sir, we were hiking and just followed the beaten path here!" They laughed and were very kind in telling us that we should not have been there because it was not safe. They rounded up the other members of our group, and we went out together.

The Chain Gang in 2014. *From left to right*: (*front row*) Michael, Holly Enk and D.J. Haralson (*middle row*) Wendy Moxley Roe and Karl K. (*back row*) Betty Erickson and Terrie Lornson. *Author's collection.*

The officers watched us leave through the holes in the fence we came through. Later, we talked about the fact that, if we had followed the others into the cells immediately, we would have missed passing the guards and possibly would have been locked in. They were there doing a daily inspection, and that was the only reason the doors were open. The thought of being locked in the old prison both amused and terrified us.

Just as we were going through the doors of the prison with the guards, a couple who had been at the original ironworks gathering drove into the parking lot in front of the prison. From the gate, they snapped a photo of us coming down the steps with the armed officers.

Who else can say they got kicked out of one of the most notorious prisons in the world? Our adventure and the incredible impressions that were made on me that day led me down a five-year path to this book. At the time, I had no idea that what I would find on my journey were explanations for the overwhelming vibe that hovers over Old Joliet Prison. In those explanations, I would learn that this massive stone fortress is so far beyond just an old prison.

Acknowledgements

First and foremost, I would like to thank my family for the support they have shown me throughout this process. My mom and dad, Rick and Gail Moxley; my daughters and their families, Erin, Sean, Tucker, Sylar, Sam and Will; my sister, Valerie; and my brother, Brian, all deserve my thanks. I am beyond blessed to have them all in my life. During the times I was ready to pull my hair out and give up, they cheered me on, all the way to the finish line.

A big thank-you and hugs also go to those of you who shared your experiences, photographs or stories with me, including David Pineda, Rob Johnson, Tony Szabelski, Jason Sherman and Neil Gibbons.

The Joliet Area Historical Museum (JAHM) staff was gracious and so very helpful during the process of putting this book together. A large number of the photographs in this book came from JAHM, and I would like to send a huge thank-you to all of the staff members for the work they did to bring life back to the Old Joliet Prison and for their help with this book.

A special thank-you goes to my go-to at the museum, curator Heather Bigeck, for the time she took to help me with any questions I had, pictures and anything else I needed.

Finally, I would like to extend a warm hug and big thank-you to Karl K., who, eight years ago, opened a door to things I wouldn't have ever dreamed possible. Wherever our paths may take us, I will always love you and be grateful that we met that day in Bachelor's Grove.

To my friends Keely Wheeler, David Pineda, Karen Paradis, Dana and Sonny, thank you for the support and love you gave me when I needed it most. Our evening chats will stay with me, always!

INTRODUCTION

What does the word *haunted* really mean? There are as many different answers to this question as there are people to ask it. Most who hear the word *haunted* immediately imagine ghosts and flying objects. To those of us with a more than slight interest in the subject, the mention of the word is enough to set off a black-hole discussion that could last for days. The word has several different meanings. These definitions are attempts to explain what is inexplicable.

For as long as people have been able to reason, we have contemplated death and what is beyond our lives here on Earth. A popular belief has always been that ghosts and paranormal activity are created by something that is left behind when a person or living being dies. Depending on religious or social beliefs, these ideas can vary widely, but we can all agree that the paranormal realm is something that is not provable beyond a doubt and that all theories can be possibilities.

As far back as the early 1800s, scientists have spent good portions of their lives developing and researching theories that would explain preternatural experiences. From the early idea that the words we speak can be recorded in the atmosphere sprang ideas of inanimate objects, buildings and places being able to absorb certain aspects of human interaction. Most of these theories also support the idea that negative emotions are the number one thing that can produce the amount of energy needed to imprint events into time and space. The bigger the trauma, the more intense the human energy produced.

In the 1960s, British archaeologist T.C. Lethbridge began researching paranormal activity as a result of things he had previously experienced in his work. He believed that there was a type of energy field between the physical and spiritual reality that acted as a medium. He also believed certain places or objects are surrounded by this field, which hold recordings of past events and are able to replay these events with the help of certain properties. Lethbridge said that places that have seen a lot of pain, suffering and death are more likely to hold these fields, as are places with high levels of humidity. Old Joliet Prison could be the definition of this theory. Its reputation for death and suffering has been known from the start, and the conditions over the years have been referred to many times as a dank, dark dungeon and a "living graveyard."

In 1972, the BBC movie titled *The Stone Tape* aired on Christmas Day. In the film, an electronics research team started working on finding a new recording medium in an old Victorian house. After seeing several "ghosts," the team decided to analyze the activity, which they believed were psychic impressions trapped in the stone walls. The film's name then became synonymous with pop culture references to residual hauntings or place memories. The theories gained more attention in 1988, when chemist Don Robbins released his book *Secret Language of Stone*. Robbins believed that certain types of minerals and crystals had the ability to absorb and store outside electrical forces, which could later be triggered by psychic aspects to be replayed as if they were movies.

Limestone has long been believed to possess these properties and has been identified as being a common trait among known haunted locations constructed of stone or near large stone quarries. Old Joliet Prison was literally carved from the land that it still sits on today. In addition to the original structure that was built mostly from limestone, it sits on a solid limestone bedrock. Broiling emotions raged inside the prison walls continuously, so surely this is a catalyst for many of the horrible events that happened there. Through my research of the prison, I found multiple reports of inmate deaths, murders and suicides inside the prison. One man, while he was working, suddenly decided that he had heard enough of the incessant chatting of the inmate working beside him. In one swift move, he hit the talking man over the head with his shovel, instantly killing him. When questioned why he had done it, the man simply shrugged his shoulders and said, "To shut him up." Violence and remorse seemed to go hand and hand in the tales that have come out of the prison through the years. Prisoners haunted by the pasts they carried with them were locked in where they were unable to avoid them.

I met David Pineda in the winter of 2020. David had spent four years inside of Old Joliet in the 1990s. When we met, this book was almost finished, and his personal stories of the place confirmed some of my thoughts and

Southeast guard tower. *Author's collection.*

theories about the prison. David said he has always seen his victims' faces. He carries them with him everywhere he goes. When he was locked up inside Old Joliet, he said he could do nothing but face what he had done. You will see this running theme popping up in many of the stories in this book.

David also spoke of the common occurrence of feeling cold spots in the prison cells, even in the stifling humidity of the summer months. On David's first night in Old Joliet, he said he was just about to fall asleep when a strong vibration swept loudly through the rows of the east cellblock's iron bars. He said it sounded as if someone very large and powerful was banging on them. No one alive or visible was causing the ruckus. He believes the victims and past inmates of Old Joliet were making their presence known. They were saying, "I am still here and will always be."

The stories I have presented in this book are some of the darkest of those that have come out of the Old Joliet Prison intermixed with some accounts of the paranormal activities that have been witnessed in and around the prison. Some are possibly magnified by the natural paranormal conductors and fueled by the hearts and consciences of guilty men.

PART I

THE HISTORY

Early photograph of Old Joliet Prison. *Courtesy of the Joliet Area Historical Museum.*

1
BUILDING A LEGEND

For several decades, the Old Joliet Prison was one of the largest prisons in the country. It was the place where the worst of the worst were sent. Those who entered through the iron gates of this massive giant were here to stay for a while—a good while. Inside the gates was a cruel, hard world of its own that showed no mercy to those who lived there. The massive structure that still stands on Collins Street in Joliet, Illinois, was built to fulfill the need for a new prison. Alton State Prison had, for some time, been having severe issues with overcrowding and deteriorating conditions. It was also very expensive to transport prisoners the many miles between the prison and the ever-growing city of Chicago, where most of the inmates came from.

Located just a few miles from the city limits, the many assets of the new prison's plot of land in Joliet, Illinois, which was originally called Stoneville, were what made the site perfect for the vision of the new Illinois State Prison. The main draw of the location was that the seventy-two acres that made up the site sat on top of solid limestone bedrock. This mass of limestone would prove beneficial in two ways. First and foremost, the land would yield a large part of the building materials that were needed. Second, the solid bedrock under the prison would make escape by tunneling out impossible. Other benefits included a natural spring on site that provided fresh water, the Chicago Alton Railroad that ran right through the property, and not too far to the west was the I&M Canal. The latter two became keys in the success of the prison in the manufacturing industry.

Aerial photograph of Old Joliet Prison that was taken around the 1930s. *Courtesy of the Joliet Area Historical Museum.*

Keynote: 1. Administration Building; 2. East Cellblock; 3. West Cellblock; 4. Hospital; 5. East Sally Port; 6. Gym; 7. 1851 Original Cell; 8. North Segregation Cells; 9. Laundry and Library; 10. Chapel and School; 11. Storage building; 12. Machine Shop; 13. Commissary; 14. Quarry; 15. Women's Prison; 16. Dining Hall; A. Southeast Guard Tower; B. Northeast Guard Tower; C. Northwest Guard Tower; D. Southwest Guard Tower.

Construction of the Joliet Penitentiary began in August 1857, and the first group of prisoners arrived at the site on January 22, 1858. A campsite was set up for them to live in while they began the grueling process of mining the limestone and building the massive complex around them. Over two years, as the prison grew, so did its population. The last group of prisoners was transferred in July of 1860, and the Alton location closed. Although the prison was then fully functional, construction was continuous throughout the rest of the 1800s.

The continuous construction was reminiscent of the infamous Winchester Mystery Mansion. Sarah Winchester, the wife of the creator of the Winchester rifle, believed that she channeled her dead husband from the afterworld soon after his death. During this communication, he said she must move from their home in New Haven, Connecticut, to San Jose, California, where she was to build a house from the ground up. Using the Winchester fortune, she was to continue construction on the house as penance for all the lives taken by a Winchester gun. The construction went on, twenty-four hours a day, for thirty-eight years. The Winchester Mansion is now a

Inmates working in the prison quarry. *Courtesy of the Joliet Area Historical Museum.*

Prison quarry. *Courtesy of the Joliet Area Historical Museum.*

The southeast guard tower, wall and hospital roof as it looks today. *Author's collection.*

museum and is said to be haunted by many of the souls who died from the family's guns. Sarah believed that the house was being built just for them. The prison, being made mostly of limestone, combined with all the other paranormal conductors the complex possesses, including the energy created by continuous construction, has an anomalous atmosphere.

The prison's giant guard towers stand in the four corners of the main structure. Fifteen acres is encircled on three sides by walls that are twenty-five feet tall and six feet wide at the base, tapering to two feet wide at the top. The fourth side that completes the enclosure consists of the administration building, which is flanked on either side by two cellblocks. The nine hundred cells split between the west and east wings are made entirely of stone and iron. No wood was used so that there was no chance of anything structural catching fire. Stone naturally holds water, especially limestone. In the summer months, it added to the stifling humidity; in the winter, the moisture would freeze, turning the cells into igloos. The original cells measured eight feet deep by four and a half feet wide by seven and a half feet tall—just barely big enough for the two prisoners each held. Modern plumbing was not installed until the 1950s. Until then, a large wooden bucket was used inside the cell when prisoners needed to relieve themselves. Each morning, before breakfast, the prisoners would take their waste buckets to a sewage pit in the yard, where they would empty them. The stench this created in the

Warden Joseph Ragen outside an original cell that still stands in the prison today. *Courtesy of the Joliet Area Historical Museum.*

yard and the cellblocks was said to be almost intolerable, especially during hot summer months.

The original plans for Joliet included a 100 cellblock for women prisoners that included its own wall. These were the first cells built, and they housed both males and females until the east cellblock in the main building was completed in 1865. The 100 cellblock remained female-only quarters for five years and housed anywhere between a dozen and twenty female inmates at a time. Overcrowding in the men's cells came to a critical point around 1870, when the prison's administration decided to utilize the unused cells in the female sector for male prisoners. Having both sexes inside the same cellhouse became a huge problem. The chaplain at the time advised the warden that something had to be done about the situation. The chaplain's plea and the continuous flow of incoming inmates spurred the warden to move all female inmates to the fourth floor of the administration building. They were kept in this location until 1896, when the women's building was built just across Colins Street.

The Women's Prison. *Author's collection.*

The prison was embroiled in controversy even before it opened officially. For the first several years of its existence, the prison was leased to and run by private individuals. The corruption that came with this type of management was so egregious that locals begged officials to take charge of the prison, which had become a cesspool of corruption, immorality and depravity. A three-man committee was appointed to choose a warden to run the prison's everyday workings. The warden would also implement a system in which private companies could submit proposals and win contracts for inmate labor. It took several years and as many new wardens for the new arrangement to work.

By 1872, Old Joliet had grown to the point of being the largest prison in the United States. Two years later, Robert W. McClaughry was appointed warden and held the position for fourteen years. McClaughry was the first warden to successfully run the prison, and he gained Old Joliet national attention for being a model institute. The prison, by this time, was running well, but the controversy over convict labor continued for some time. Some argued that the use of cheap convict labor took jobs from hardworking men. Others praised the program, saying that it boosted the city's economy. The *Joliet Signal* openly opposed the use of convict labor. In 1870, it printed an article that gave exact numbers of what was being

Above: Inmates in the prison hospital in the early twentieth century. *Courtesy of the Joliet Area Historical Museum.*

Left: Current photograph of the front of the prison's hospital building. *Courtesy of the Joliet Area Historical Museum.*

produced by the prison in one month: 359,000 cigars, 6,456 brooms, 5,519 barrels, 270 chairs, 127 cases of shoes, 18,245 castings, 250 wagons, 10 grain drills, 242 cultivators, 92 wheelbarrows, 1,388 army tents, 7,500 feet of dressed stone, 26,884 feet of cut stone, 90 yards of bridge stone, 239 cords of rubble stone, 41 harness sets, 132 fly nets and 864 horse halters. The numbers clearly show how the manufactured goods produced at the prison cut into local competition's business. The end of convict labor for production came by the turn of the century.

The need for a large facility to house the many sick and dying inmates grew along with the prison's population. The on-ground, inmate hospital would be completed in 1895. At the time, 70 percent of deaths in the prison were due to tuberculosis. Known back then as consumption, tuberculosis had killed one in seven humans alive until that point. The cure was not found and deemed viable for human consumption until 1949. Tuberculosis was thought to be genetic and was often treated by sending infected individuals to a sanitorium for rest and sunshine, which was believed back then to alter the disease. Obviously, this was not an option for inmates in a maximum-security state prison, such as Joliet. Inmates would be moved to the hospital building once they were too sick to function in the prison population. The tuberculosis bacteria slowly ate the flesh of the lungs from the inside out, causing the infected to slowly waste away until they perished. Hundreds of men died a slow, painful death from tuberculosis in the prison hospital building; this does not include how many others died from different ailments or injuries. The hospital is said to be one of the most active buildings, aside from the solitary confinement cells, at the prison. When left inside one of the hospital rooms on an X-ray table, a member of the *Ghost Adventures* television show ran out of the room, terrified of a large black mass that he encountered during the filming of an episode at the prison. Other reported phenomena in the hospital building include unexplained noises and accounts of full-body apparitions.

The following decade dragged by, with inmates being kept busy by walking in line in the prison yard. It was not until 1913 that changes came; that year, modernist and former Joliet mayor Edmund M. Allen took the position of warden. He immediately began making changes to the prison's strict rules and procedures. He allowed the prisoners to receive letters regularly, the striped uniforms were replaced by a lighter summer ensemble in the warmer months and the no-talking rule was lifted. Instead of punishing inmates by placing them in isolation in solitary cells, Allen began restricting privileges from prisoners when they broke rules. This method proved to be successful,

Inmate with a donkey cart on the Honor Farm during Warden Edmund M. Allen's administration. *Courtesy of the Joliet Area Historical Museum.*

as the number of inmates in solitary confinement cells was cut in half during Warden Allen's administration.

Allen also implemented a new honor system and established a farm nearby that went by the same name. The Honor Farm was located a few miles away on two thousand acres that had been purchased for the Stateville Facility, which was built later. The Honor Farm was fully functional, and the fresh food that was produced there was used to feed the prisoners. This saved the prison money and supplied nutritional meals for prisoners. Those who worked and lived on the farm were selected due to their exceptionally good behavior and trustworthy status.

Sadly, Warden Allen's time and success at the prison was cut short when he resigned in the latter part of 1915. In July of that year, his wife, Odette, was murdered on prison grounds. At the time, law stated that the warden had to live on site. The warden's quarters at Old Joliet were on the upper floors of the administration building. Some believed his laissez faire regime inside the prison was to blame for her death, as it had come by the hand of one of the trusted inmates who served the Allen family personally. Warden Allen's successor, Michael Zimmer, tried to continue the reform work that Allen had started, but he only lasted two years at the position.

In early June of 1917, prisoners rioted and nearly destroyed the prison. Unable to regain control, the administration called in the National Guard. They arrived just in time. Seven buildings were already engulfed in flames, and the prisoners were just about to get through one of the sally ports by ramming a railroad car through it. The National Guardsmen were able to get the crowd under control, but nothing was the same afterward. Governor Frank Lowden appointed a new warden, E.J. Murphy, a few days later. Murphy was known to be a strict disciplinarian and proved his reputation once he took over the prison. All inmates' personal items were removed from cells, visiting and writing privileges were canceled and the strict no-talking rule was put back into place. Due to the combination of Mrs. Allen's widely publicized murder and the massive damage done by the rioting, it would be a long time before prison reform was even thought of again.

It was also in 1917 that construction began on Stateville Prison, which was intended to close Old Joliet immediately. Stateville opened in 1925, but things did not go as planned. The two prisons continued to operate side by side for several decades due to the ever-growing population of criminals coming through their gates. As the prison moved into the raging 1920s and 1930s, the gangs on the inside were pretty much running the place, and inmate violence was at an all-time high—so much so that it was making newspaper headlines across the country. At one point in 1930, a Minnesota newspaper published a small story about Author Reid, who was serving a life sentence for attempted murder and won his parole by informing officials of an inmate escape plot to blow up a wall. Two years later, Reid was arrested for stealing coal. The theft violated his parole and reinstated his original sentence. After his arrest, he literally collapsed in the holding cell, stating before that if they sent him back to Joliet, it would surely be a death sentence. He was shown mercy by the courts and remanded to a different facility.

In March of 1931, a riot broke out in the old prison dining room, and it flowed over to Stateville four days later. The dining hall, kitchen and several shops were damaged by fires at the old facility. The inmates raged for hours before being subdued with tear gas and gunfire. One inmate was killed, and three others were seriously wounded at this time. The riots came just a month after prison officials learned of an escape plot that was to be executed at the end of February (detailed in Section IV, Chapter 3). Instead of posting guards inside the prison to capture the escapees, officials placed armed guards across the street at the local restaurant parking lot and instructed them to shoot any prisoners coming over the wall. This is precisely what happened.

Two dog statues sitting in the field on the west side of the prison in 2014. *Author's collection.*

Three inmates who were attempting to climb over the wall from the east cell tower were all gunned down with machine guns. Two died instantly, and the third died hours later.

Joseph E. Ragen was appointed as warden of the Joliet prisons in 1935, after the governor removed Frank Whipp from that position. The gang activity and lack of control inside the prison had come to critical points. Escape attempts and violent deaths were mounting, and the heat was on. Officials wanted to know why so many were dying in and around the prison.

Warden Ragen's dogs were his constant companions during his time at Joliet. Two dog statues sat for many years outside in the prison yard. Legend says that they were modeled after Ragen's dogs, Duke and Mickey. The statues were still sitting outside the prison as of 2014 but are now gone.

One of the first things Ragen did as warden was a thorough walkthrough of both prisons. In his journal, he described the old prison as its own little world, with no structure or authority from guards at all. Prisoners were allowed the freedom to roam the grounds freely and at will. The prison yard was filled with makeshift shacks that housed obvious moonshine stills

The dog statues in the prison yard. The statues are said to be modeled after Warden Ragen's dogs that were his constant companions during his administration. *Courtesy of the Joliet Area Historical Museum.*

and growing marijuana plants. Some were bold enough to display signs that said, "No Officers." The convicts had control over the entire prison, except the prison wall.

The first thing Ragen did was establish who the leaders of the gangs were and move them to other facilities in the state in the middle of the night without warning. Ragen then continued to clean up the prisons little by little. He was eventually recognized as having one of the most successful penal careers. In March of 1936, he put the entire prison band in solitary confinement for a few days with a diet of bread and water. The band had been denied their usual snack after a broadcasted Sunday night performance, so they decided to protest loudly by yelling and using their instruments. The warden cracked down on them to show that all who disobey would be dealt with.

In 1943, the state announced that it would make good on its original plan to close the old prison and transfer all the prisoners to Stateville, but World War II and Warden Ragen had different plans. Instead of closing the prison, Ragen

Right: An inmate's cell in the east cellblock in May 2014. *Photograph by Karl K.*

Below: East cellblock in May 2014. *Photograph by Karl K.*

procured government contracts to put the prisoners back in prison shops to manufacture uniforms and other military necessities. The prison once again became a model institute under the direction of Warden Ragen.

The early 1950s brought a total renovation to the east and west cellblocks. Inmates finally had running water and modern plumbing in their cells, but the cells remained dark and damp as they were before. Warden Ragen left his position for good in 1961. For the next few years, Warden Frank Tate took the position, but after Ragen's exit, the prison was never run the same way again.

In the typical style of the 1960s, peace, love and protests came to Old Joliet. Charles Thomas, a twenty-five-year-old prisoner convicted of rape, learned that if he climbed the water tower in the prison yard, no one would come after him. His first escape attempt in September of 1965 ended after seventeen hours because he was hungry and thirsty. A photograph of him sitting on the catwalk of the water tower during his second escape attempt made local newspapers. He had scratched his name, prisoner number and an invitation to the governor to visit on the water tower before commencing his "sit-in." Warden Frank Tate said they were just going to let Charles be until he came down. Charles's cellmate informed the warden that, this time, the man had climbed the water tower loaded with supplies of peanut butter, candy bars and cigarettes. He had even rigged a cup and string to be able to dip drinking water from a small door in the tower. Charles lasted eleven days on top of the water tower before a pouring rain forced him to come down. He was given a hearty breakfast and taken directly to the hospital for psychiatric evaluation.

It was during this time that the prison began functioning as a reception and classification center for Northern Illinois. New prisoners stayed for no more than a few weeks before being transferred to their final location. Approximately twenty thousand inmates were filtered through Old Joliet per year, in addition to the prison's general population.

In 1969, inmate Richard Lawson was serving a sentence in Stateville of two to six years for possession of marijuana. Having secured a job as a photographer for the prison, Lawson discovered hundreds of glass-plate negatives of the prison around the turn of the century. Lawson was finally released in 1977. He had all the remaining glass negatives given to the Illinois State Museum in Springfield, Illinois. In 1982, Lawson published the photographs in a journal with a history of the prison.

The seventies brought with them all the rage and violence going on in the outside world. An uprising occurred in 1975, when a group of about 200 inmates, made up of members of active Chicago gangs, took over the entire west cellblock. They were able to take 12 hostages, including several correctional officers. The outbreak came after the current warden announced his plan to move 3 gang leaders to Menard Prison. The state police showed up soon after the unrest began, fully garbed in riot gear. Tear gas was used, after which police were able to take back seven of the eight cell tiers; 2 hostages were released, and 130 of the original 200 rebellious inmates surrendered. The remaining 70 prisoners were holed up in one cell tier with the remaining 10 hostages. In order to secure the hostages' release and end the situation, the warden promised over a radio broadcast that he would not transfer the 3 individuals as originally planned. All hostages were unharmed aside from minor scrapes and bruises. Twenty-nine-year-old inmate Herbert Catlett was not as lucky. Shortly after the uprising began, Catlett walked into the cells that were being held in the hopes of reasoning with the riotous prisoners. For his attempt at peace making, he was brutally stabbed to death.

In its last years, the prison was used as a reception and classification center. Inmates spent a few weeks in Old Joliet before it was determined which Illinois facility they would spend the bulk of their sentence in. Once they were processed and their court dates were finished, they were transported to their determined institute.

In February of 2002, the last of the inmates were transferred from the old prison to Stateville, and its doors were closed for good. Old Joliet sat quietly for sixteen years. In 2018, the Joliet Area Historical Museum and the City of Joliet began giving tours and having events in the prison to raise money for its restoration. They have come far but still have a long way to go to meet their goal of making the Old Joliet Prison a fully functional independent tour site. To help the continued restoration effort or take a tour, please visit the museum's website at www.jolietmuseum.org.

2
PUNISHMENT AND CONDITIONS

The mere mention of Old Joliet was enough to strike fear in the hearts of the hardest men. Its reputation for being one of the hardest places to serve time was well known. On Thanksgiving Day in 1883, a reporter for the *Cincinnati Enquirer* visited the Old Joliet Prison. He made the journey by train from Chicago, which led him to the train stop that was almost at the prison doors. He interviewed the man in charge of the small station, who, when asked about men arriving to serve their sentence, said, "I've seen any number of them become weak at heart when they get off here; they stand and look like wild men and burst into tears and almost have to be dragged up to the prison."

Incoming inmates had a very hard time adjusting to the difficult lifestyle on the inside. Once a prisoner entered the prison to serve his sentence, he was basically cut off from the outside world. He was permitted to send one letter once a week. Once every eight weeks, he could receive a visitor. Inmates were not permitted to talk to each other at all until around the turn of the century. While working, inmates were to pay strict attention to their tasks and not look at or communicate with others in any way unless it was necessary. Work was a big—and probably the best—part of the prisoners' days. They spent about fourteen hours in cells that were barely big enough for one man, let alone the two or sometimes three that overcrowding sometimes made necessary. No work on Sunday left them in their cells for the entire day, except for a couple of hours in which they could attend church services if they wished to.

The pillory and whipping post at Joliet Prison around 1874. *Courtesy of the Joliet Area Historical Museum.*

The original cells were four feet wide by seven feet tall by eight feet deep. Made of solid slabs of stone, they had no windows, and their only ventilation was a pipe in the wall. There were two cellblocks, with cells laid out in tiers in the center of the building. One hundred cells, which sat back to back in each tier, rose five stories high in the west cellblock and four stories high in the east cellblock. Fourteen feet lay between the cell doors and the outer wall, so little if any natural light came through. An iron bunk bed, just wide enough to hold a human being, occupied half of the cell space. The bedding consisted of a corn husk–stuffed mattress, a straw pillow, sheets and a coarse wool blanket. Inmates were provided with a shelf for books, a small wooden stool, a stone water jug and a slop bucket for waste. Modern-day plumbing did not come to the cells until the 1950s, during a total renovation of both cellblocks. The combination of the smells of a huge raw sewage pit in the yard behind the cellblocks, raw sewage in the slop buckets and hundreds of sweaty men enclosed in a place with no ventilation was said to be so horrible that it stayed with them even after they left. Baths were only given once a week during the summer months and every two weeks during winter. Fifteen tubs in a small bathing room were used by all 1,500 inmates to bathe. In order to get through all of them in an efficient amount of time, some were forced to bathe two at a time.

Inmates began their days when a bell rang at 5:45 a.m. They had fifteen minutes to get ready to exit their cells and march to the kitchen, where they were given a breakfast of coffee, bread and hash (a mixture of bacon, beef and potatoes). On the way to breakfast, they would each empty their waste buckets in an open sewage pit in the yard. Meals were eaten in the cells before 1903, when the dining hall was built and communal dinning was introduced. At 6:45 a.m. each day, prisoners left their cells for their work assignments. Approximately four hundred men crossed the road each day to work in the quarry. The rest worked within the prison's walls in one of the many shops that were leased by private individuals or in positions that were necessary to run the prison. When it was time for prisoners to move anywhere outside of their cells, they were lined up and moved together in lockstep, lined in single file, with their left hand on the shoulder of the man in front of them. They would then proceed to march this way to their intended destination.

Until 1875, prisoners were only allowed outside for one hour once a year. That same year, the tradition of holding a Fourth of July celebration for the prisoners began. The prison was decorated with flags and banners, and prisoners could roam the yard to talk and compete in athletic games with each other. A hearty meal was served, including dessert, and afterward, there was entertainment. It was one of the only reprieves from the monotony that was their lives. The Independence Day celebration was so popular with the inmates that it moved one man to write a poem about the day. Sundays were the opportunity for inmates to go to church if they wished or to lounge about in their cells.

Prisoners walking in lockstep inside Joliet Prison around 1874. *Courtesy of the Joliet Area Historical Museum.*

Daily life inside the prison was physically and mentally straining. The conditions described thus far were hard enough to bear, but when an inmate broke the rules, they were taken to a whole new level of hell. In the prison's earlier years, punishments were brutal and consisted of whipping or being locked in the stockades or solitary confinement. For those who continued to flagrantly break rules after other punishments were ineffective, there was the hole. Holes only a few feet wide and about six feet deep were dug in the ground of the prison yard; then, prisoners were thrown in, the holes were covered, and they were left for days with no food or water. As one can imagine, many did not survive this punishment. In those days, there were no laws protecting prisoners; once they were inside, they were at the sole mercy of those in charge.

Paranormal investigator Jason Sherman was one of the first to privately investigate Old Joliet in 2018, when the Joliet Area Historical Museum began giving tours of the prison to raise money for its restoration. He experienced rocks being thrown at him in the prison yard repeatedly throughout the time he spent investigating and giving tours at the prison. He also heard the sounds of cell doors closing multiple times. With each occurrence, Jason would search the area for the culprit of the incidents, but none could ever be found. One particular night, after being at the prison for a long period of time, he said he arrived home and took off a crystal bracelet he had worn as protection during his investigations that night. In the middle of the night, he heard a loud splintering noise. When he turned the light on, the bracelet was on the bedroom floor, shattered into tiny pieces. He said it was as if the energy absorbed by the bracelet that night in the prison could not be contained, and it literally burst the crystal pieces apart.

Prison laws began to change with the century. The harsher forms of punishment were done away with, and the common punishment became solitary confinement. A prisoner who was being reprimanded was locked in one of the one hundred segregation cells for a period of time, depending on the severity of their offense and how long it took them to submit and behave. For up to twelve hours, they would be cuffed in a standing position to the iron bars of their cell door. If they continued to be loud or unruly, a solid iron door would be shut, and the prisoner would be engulfed in dark silence. They were uncuffed for the remainder of the day if they were behaving, but they only had the cold, hard stone floor to sit or sleep on. Once a day, they were fed a meager portion of bread and water. It did not take most very long to give in. Inmates who left solitary after long periods in the dark cells were said to have been pictures of living death. Some inmates who were taken from solitary confinement were so weak that they had to spend a few days recovering in the prison hospital. The segregation cells were home to the raging unruly. As in any prison, there were those who were always in trouble and being thrown into solitary.

Once inmates were in the solitary cells, away from all other prisoners, they were more likely to be victims of excessive force and brutality. Many questionable deaths occurred in the segregation cells at Old Joliet. It was not until the 1970s that the law required an autopsy for any inmate death on prison grounds. Before then, it was up to officials' discretion. There were many, especially during the prison's first fifty years, who died and were simply buried without any concern as to what had caused their death.

In 1878, an inmate who was being punished in solitary was handcuffed to his cell door and started yelling loudly and cursing in the middle of the night. Using a part of a broom as a makeshift gag, a guard stuffed the contraption in the prisoner's mouth and held it in place with leather straps on either side of his head that connected behind his neck. Each time the prisoner started getting loud, the gag was tightened until he stopped.

Current view of the solitary confinement cells. *Photograph by Rob Johnson.*

This happened several times over a period of about thirty-six hours. On the afternoon of the second day, the guards found the man dead in his cell. The autopsy revealed that he had died from pulmonary apoplexy due to screaming with the gag in his mouth. Essentially, he screamed so intensely that the veins in his lungs ruptured, and he slowly drowned in his own blood. The guard in charge of the prisoner that day testified that he had flogged the man once and gagged him three times that day, all on orders that came from above. During the inquest into the prisoner's death, all the prison officials denied that any such order was ever given. Two guards were fired, and other officials were mildly reprimanded, including the warden. The incident incited local newspapers to publicly call out the prison administration for what they saw as superiors using underlings as scapegoats for their bad decisions. It was a problem that plagued Old Joliet repeatedly. The stories of questionable suicides that happened in the solitary unit are detailed in this book's later chapters.

In October 2018, researcher Tony Szabelski and his group conducted a paranormal investigation in the segregation cells of the Old Joliet Prison using what is known in para culture as the Devil's toybox. The box is mirrored on all six of its internal sides; the theory behind the box is that its mirrors are portals or doors to other dimensions and having them reflect at each other inside the box creates a continuous loop of energy that spirits are drawn to. Using the mirrors as a door, the spirits cross over but are then trapped in the box. Once the spirit is trapped in the box, it is said you can hear voices and noises coming from inside. Tony and his group were using

The painted sign on the floor of the solitary confinement cells. *Courtesy of the Joliet Area Historical Museum.*

a version of the box that contains a small microphone in the bottom, giving real-time amplified communication with the trapped spirit. What the group heard come out of the box that night sounded like a pack of wolves howling at the moon. The segregation cells at Old Joliet Prison have been called some of the closest places to Hell there have ever been. Maybe Tony's group that night captured the nearby baying hounds of Hell's gate.

3

THE SINGING CONVICT GHOST

Long abandoned and forgotten now, a cemetery known as Monkey Hill sat about a quarter of a mile away from the Old Joliet Prison. Prisoners who had died on prison grounds and had their bodies left unclaimed were buried here. There are possibly one thousand men buried in the cemetery, where the only markers were coffin-shaped planks of wood with simple names and convict numbers. The name Monkey Hill was attached to it at some point many years ago but was not its official name. It is currently not exactly known when or why it started being called Monkey Hill, but the name stuck, and it is still referred to by that name. It was an active cemetery until 1925, when Stateville Prison was opened, and inmates were buried on a plot of land close to the newer facility. The new cemetery is the Illinois State Penitentiary (ISP) Cemetery on Caton Farm Road in Joliet; it is often mistaken for Monkey Hill. They are, in fact, two separate cemeteries. Monkey Hill no longer exists as a cemetery. Its wooden markers disintegrated long ago and disappeared back into the earth. The location is known by some, but the site is no longer accessible to the public.

In July of 1932, the country was held captive by the story of a singing ghost that had appeared in the convict cemetery. What began with a local fisherman's encounter with a disembodied voice on his walk home through the cemetery one evening eventually turned into crowds of thousands of people gathering at the cemetery to hear a nightly performance by a ghost. At the time, Monkey Hill Cemetery was just beyond the backyards of a small neighborhood called Fairmont Hill. Ghost stories had circulated around the

Burial in Monkey Hill Cemetery. Convicts who died on the prison's grounds and were unclaimed after death were buried here until around 1925. *Courtesy of the Joliet Area Historical Museum.*

cemetery for as many years as it had existed. It was the place that locals always walked past with sideways glances and that kids dared each other to enter. When the singing sensation was at its peak, newspaper reporters interviewed locals who had experienced the activity in person in the cemetery.

Two years before the singing ghost made his appearance, a full-body apparition was seen by two local men while they were walking past the cemetery in full daylight one summer afternoon on their way home from work. Dressed in a full Confederate gray Civil War soldier's uniform, a man was sitting on top of one of the graves in the center of the cemetery. As they both stood there, too stunned to say anything or move, the figure disappeared before their eyes. The prison was built just as the Civil War was beginning, and it is believed that the prison was used to hold Confederate prisoners of war. It is also believed that some of those men are buried in the convict cemetery. Several members of the local neighborhood also reported seeing a white-mist form floating among the headstones before slowly dissipating. Strange noises were commonly heard coming from the cemetery by those who lived close by. The sounds were described as animal like but not like any animal they had ever heard.

The sensation in the summer of 1932 began one night while a local fisherman was walking home from work. His shortcut took him through the old convict cemetery, and as he passed through it, he heard a voice ask him, "Any luck today?" When he turned to reply, there was no one there. Startled, he quickly made his way home, shaken by the incident. From then on, he took the long way home.

The Dudek family was the first to hear the singing voice. The backyard of the family's home bordered the convict cemetery. Mrs. Dudek heard it first, a deep male voice singing what she thought were Latin hymns. She called her daughter to come to the yard, and they both investigated the area with a flashlight. They found nothing and no one. The next night, Mr. Dudek and his son repeated the same routine after hearing the voice singing shortly before midnight. The men did a more detailed search but came up with the same results. Every night after that, for nearly a month, just around midnight, a "ghost" would start to sing and would continue its performance for over an hour. The newspapers caught wind of the story, and soon, articles were being run in papers across the country. What began as some locals showing up out of curiosity was suddenly people pouring in by the thousands from miles around. Despite the huge number of people gathering in the cemetery, no one could find the source of the enchanting voice. At one point, a crowd, desperate for the slightest clue as to what was going on, dug up a corner of the cemetery, where they thought the voice was coming from. To their disappointment, their efforts were for nothing, as that is exactly what they found.

Anthony Grohar, the neighborhood grocer, and George Penmar were a part of the group of diggers and had heard the ghost sing several times. In an interview by a local newspaper, they described their experience with the phantom singer. "Once, while the voice was issuing from the graveyard," said Grohar, "I turned my automobile headlights upon the graves. The song kept on, but it came from a different part of the cemetery. As I'd move my lights, the ghost would jump one flight ahead of them." The fact that huge groups of people were searching for a source or explanation for the phenomenon and finding nothing only fueled the rumors that the singing was indeed a voice from another world. The popular theory was that the ghost was that of a disgruntled convict who had been executed for a crime he did not commit.

An article that was written on the earliest record of an execution in the city of Joliet tells the story of a man named George Chase—or at least that is what he said his name was. There was no relative or record ever found to confirm his identity. George was a horse thief; in the 1860s, that was the equivalent of grand theft auto today. For his crime, he was sentenced to serve several years in Joliet. A disturbed man, he did not do well once he was serving his time on the inside. He was consistently insubordinate and was a habitual rule breaker, for which he was repeatedly punished. By the spring of 1864, George had served two years. He found himself once again in solitary confinement. This time, the dark isolation was not working. He continued to rebel and not cooperate with guards, to the point that they decided a more severe punishment was needed. They immobilized him by putting him in irons; cuffs, leg armor and chains were brought to the cell by two guards and the deputy warden, Joseph Clark. Clark unlocked the cell, and Chase stepped out into the hall. Chase then threw a very large rock that he had managed to sneak in from the quarry at the deputy warden. The rock struck Clark in the head, where it left a quarter-sized hole. The deputy warden lingered in limbo for two weeks before succumbing to his injuries.

Chase was then convicted of his murder and subsequently received the death sentence. He spent a year and a half on death row before reaching his execution date. Chase heartily proclaimed his innocence all along, even in the end. As they lowered the hood on his head to prepare him for his execution, he was quoted in the newspaper as saying, "I'm not ready for that yet. I'm as innocent a man as any of you. I am as innocent a man as any in the United States. I admit that hanging is justice. But hanging for a thing a man ain't guilty of and can't prove I am guilty of is another thing. It ain't justice." His last words were: "Gentlemen, I am to be slaughtered." Being the first execution in Joliet, the "gallows" were makeshift and erected in the hallway of the Will County Jail. Chase was seated in a chair with the noose around his neck. When the call was given, sandbags were dropped to the floor below, and Chase was rocketed five feet into the air, toward the ceiling and "eternity," as a present guard was quoted as saying. It is a dark enough story without the horror of what happened next.

Chase was pronounced dead and taken down approximately twenty minutes later. First, a phrenologist (a scientist who studies lumps on heads to determine mental traits) made a plaster cast of his head. The doctors then *removed* his head to study it for any indication of criminal behavior. When they found nothing out of the ordinary or interesting, they gave the head back to the phrenologist, who went on to display George's head and use it in lectures. George's headless body was buried in the convict cemetery called Monkey Hill. George was an angry man to the end, and he had convinced himself he was an innocent who was being unjustly murdered. One can only assume that he would not have been happy about his head traveling the country or his body being buried headless in a convict's grave.

George Chase was executed on July 27, 1866; on the same date sixty-six years later, officials announced that they had solved the singing ghost mystery. The singing had started during the anniversary of the last days that George had spent sitting on death row, waiting to be hanged. The number coincidence is odd as well; Chase was hanged in 1866, and it was sixty-six years later that the singing ghost made its appearance.

George's story was detailed in the *Chicago Tribune* when it occurred, and it was most likely told as local prison lore over the years. By the time the singing ghost made its appearance, it had morphed into something a little different with each telling, as local legends tend to do. When the sensation in the cemetery started in 1932, it was not long before the story of a disgruntled convict executed for a crime he didn't commit was attached to the singing spectral. If you, like some, believe that, when we die, we are forgiven of all our bad deeds to live as our perfect self in the next life, then the connection of headless George to the singing ghost could make sense. Maybe he was a happy, whole soul in the afterworld that came back for a while to sing sorrowful songs in remorse for his wasted life—or maybe he was just looking for his head.

The community, for the most part, was enthralled with the idea that an ethereal being was putting on such a show for them. Local business owners had no problem with people pouring in from out of town because with the people came money that was spent in the local economy. A large group of people with more conservative beliefs in such things believed the voice was something evil, and some were hysterically frightened. One woman was convinced that the world was coming to an end and that the singing ghost was the herald of Hell and the cemetery was Hell's gate. Reverend John Dvorovny of the Trinity Evangelical Church near the cemetery said that he was at an utter loss as to how to console the droves of people who were coming to him seeking solace, so he consulted his superiors as to what he or they could do. They, too, were at a loss.

When crowds start gathering in an out-of-the-way spot, trouble always finds its way into the mix. A once rarely used dirt road had lines of cars driving and parking for miles. Thousands of feet trampled once overgrown weeds and grass, and a trail of trash was left behind nightly. The crowds were getting out of hand. The cemetery had become a full-blown entertainment venue, complete with hot dog and popcorn vendors. A gang of delinquent teenagers decided to get in on the money train and blocked off certain areas of the road close to the cemetery. The hoodlums stood at the roadblocks and intimidated people into paying to park or enter. As the situation was starting to get out of hand and no explanation or end was in sight, officials had had enough. The local sheriff had become beyond annoyed with the chaos it was creating and decided to do something. He gathered a posse of seventy-five armed men and set off for the cemetery after dark to wait. For hours, nothing happened, no one was found, no explanation was discovered and, to beat it all, there was no singing. A few stragglers that had stayed behind reported that the ghost made his appearance after the last of the mob left around 3:00 a.m.

By then, the novelty of the singing episodes had begun to wear off. The performances were less frequent, and they were starting later at night. A few days later, officials at the prison announced that they had solved the mystery. The singing ghost was none other than inmate William Chrysler, who oversaw the late-night maintenance of the not-so-near sub pumps in the prison's quarries. Chrysler confessed that he sang Lithuanian folk songs in English late at night while he worked the lonely job at the quarries. He told reporters, "It's kinda spooky around here. I usually sing something like 'Rock of Ages' or 'Onward, Christian Soldiers' to cheer myself up." After hearing from a guard about the sensation his singing was causing in the cemetery, Chrysler said he would sing purposely for the crowd, humbled by the attention. When those in search of the location of the voice came around, he simply hid in the bushes to avoid detection. The explanation given by officials was that the sound was reverberating off the limestone walls and carried perfectly a quarter of a mile away. This seemed to be a logical explanation that satisfied most, and the phenomenon stopped as abruptly as it started. Sounds like a cut-and-dry case, right? But was it just as simple as that? There are a few holes in the story, and some things just don't add up.

If it was Mr. Chrysler singing, how could his singing have been heard but not the very large and very loud sub pumps? Dylan Clearfield brought up this topic in his book *Chicagoland Ghosts*, which was published in 1997. The backyard of the home Dylan grew up in bordered the field where the convict cemetery was located. Clearfield's parents were lifetime Joliet residents as well and had experienced the craze of the singing ghost firsthand. He also interviewed his friends' parents and relatives who had also grown up in the neighborhood. They were able to give details about events that were not reported in the newspapers or that were not common knowledge.

At the very end, just before officials came forward with the singing quarry worker explanation, a Catholic priest was brought in to bless the cemetery and perform an exorcism. This was not usually something that was done, but on top of the chaos caused by the thrill seekers and delinquents, the church deemed it appropriate in order to help the situation for those in the neighborhood who were so frightened that they were not leaving their homes. Whether they were more scared of the ghost or the bad people it had drawn near their homes was a tossup.

William Chrysler was due for parole two weeks after he made his claim that he was the ghostly singer. At the time of the singing ghost hype, Warden Frank Whipp was in charge. Four years later, in 1936, Warden Joseph Ragen stepped in when Whipp was forced out of the job by the then-current governor. Ragen's diary gives firsthand accounts of what he encountered on his first walkthrough of the old prison after taking the position of warden. He noted that the only control the guards had was over the wall. Inside those walls, inmates lived and ruled in their own little world. Marijuana was grown openly, and moonshine stills were out bubbling in the prison yard as if they were everyday businesses. Small shacks dotted the scene; they were erected out of scrap materials and had signs boldly stating "NO OFFICERS" on their doors. The inmates there did what they wanted.

Is it too far of a stretch to think that the Chrysler story could have been fabricated to satisfy the press and deflect unwanted attention from an administration that was not just poorly run but blatantly turning a blind eye to obvious illegal activity? Chrysler would not have objected to the deception, as he did not want to upset his chances of parole. After the singing quarry worker explanation was made public, professional musicians and ventriloquists were interviewed. The task of throwing a voice over that distance was said by all of them to be impossible, even for a master of ventriloquism, which Chrysler was not.

Chrysler's explanation for being able to avoid the throngs of spectators searching by hiding in bushes was bogus as well. There was nothing in the quarry where he was working other than rocks and dust—there were no bushes. William Chrysler was granted his parole from Joliet weeks after his short stint there as a ghost. In November of that year, a Chicago stage manager booked him to perform in front of an audience at one of his clubs in the Chicago loop. Whether the performance ever happened is unknown. Chrysler obviously did not maintain the five minutes of fame he had gained while in prison, and the news of his upcoming performance was the last report of him or the singing ghost for many years.

The cemetery slowly vanished back into Mother Earth, undetectable. The neighborhood has since changed, as has the world around it, and the only thing remaining of the sensation that rocked Joliet in the summer of 1932 is the story.

PART II

THE PEOPLE

Southwest corner towers of Old Joliet Prison. *Photograph by Karl K.*

4

FAMOUS PRISONERS

Like most large state maximum-security institutions, Joliet had its fair share of celebrity inmates. In later years, the old facility was used as a state processing center for inmates. They were processed and then held at the old prison until they could be transferred to their destination facility. All inmates in Stateville were also processed through the old prison before being transferred the few miles down the road.

The name John Wayne Gacy needs no introduction to most. In December of 1978, police found thirty-one bodies of young men in different stages of decomposition buried in the crawl space of Gacy's home in Norridge, Illinois. After his arrest, he spent about twenty-one hours inside Old Joliet before being moved to Pontiac Correctional Facility, which was located about an hour south of Joliet. Gacy was said to have been treated in the Old Joliet Prison hospital shortly before his execution in May of 1994. The popular television series *Ghost Adventures* did an hour-long special in 2019 on Old Joliet Prison. The episode featured prison photographer Rob Johnson, and he told his story of walking in the hospital alone one day when he suddenly encountered a very large shadow man in a doorway. Johnson felt the anomaly as much as he saw it. He described the figure as menacing and said it made him feel as if he was not welcome there.

The *Ghost Adventures* crew later investigated the prison hospital for themselves. One member was left alone inside one of the hospital rooms lying on an old X-ray table. He ran from the room in terror after he saw and felt heavy pressure from a black form near his head. Out of breath, he told the rest of the crew that he felt something like what Rob Johnson had experienced some time before. The crew then theorized that Gacy was such a powerful form of evil that his simple presence was enough to leave his mark inside the prison's walls. This theory seems to fit right in with others discussed earlier about the prison being a hotbed of activity due to the many paranormal conductors it possesses. With limestone having the ability to absorb and hold human energies like a recording, what would happen when a human with super energy was encased in it? Did Gacy's mere presence leave a mark?

Over the years, there have been many Joliet prisoners in the news. The subjects of the following stories were some of the more sensational headliners who left their imprints on the prison.

Louis A. Gourdain

Louis A. Gourdain was a classic case of a haunted man. He was a man haunted by his need to live in a world that was a web of lies and manipulation. He made millions through lottery scams in Louisiana and New York, taking money from hardworking people who barely made ends meet. His multiple arrests always ended with the charges being dismissed due to technicalities. The laws mandating lotteries were, in those years, in the early stages of development. Nonetheless, his arrests exposed his scams, and he would then have to flee to a new location to begin again.

Eventually, he moved to Chicago, and in 1905, he was again arrested on charges of running an illegal lottery. During his trial, he was the picture of a repentant man. He expressed deep remorse for his wrongdoings with grand theatrics, and he cried to the jury that any punishment they deemed fit, he would accept without pause. He was sentenced to four and a half years in Joliet. A few days after surrendering himself to the prison, he was told that there would be a new trial. Due to the new circumstances, he was to be moved to Cook County pending his appeal. This threw Gourdain into quite a frenzy. He told authorities that the documents he needed to get the appeal had been forged, and he refused to be transferred. Frustrated, the family was eventually able to bond him out until the appeal, releasing him from Joliet. He didn't seem to have a real issue with this, and he went home quietly. It was speculated at the time that, being the conman that he was, he was scared to death of running into those he had scammed in the Cook County facility.

It was after his release that his bizarre obsession with getting himself back into the prison to complete his sentence began. Gourdain began showing up at the gates of the old prison, demanding to be let back in. Each time, he caused a huge scene, and each time, they turned him away. At one point, the warden himself dragged Gourdain from the prison gates to the street and told him to go home and await the court proceedings. His story soon made newspaper headlines across the country after he invited a group of reporters to his home for a lavish dinner. He gave the reporters a sensational, heartfelt speech about honor and how he must be allowed to serve out his sentence as penance for what he had done. His continued pleas through the media and in person were repeatedly ignored.

His failed attempts to get back inside the prison did not stop his madness; they seemed to fuel it. He decided that if they would not let him back in, he would build his own private mini prison as an annex, right next to the real one. Inside this mini prison, he would follow the same lifestyle as he would if he were on the inside, serving his term. He even sketched blueprints for the construction of his DIY prison. The press entertained him by running his story because it was so strange, but the more attention they gave him, the more elaborate his plot for self-imprisonment became. He began making plans to travel to Washington, D.C., to petition the government to let him serve his time one way or the other. Part of these plans included moving his family to Joliet to be near the prison. Gourdain chose a guard employed by the prison who lived nearby to place his family there.

The truth of his background was discovered after his public media display. The *Cincinnati Tribune*'s front-page headline on August 12, 1906, read "GOURDAIN LUNATIC CRIMINAL." The article went on to describe, in detail, exactly how Gourdain, who was thought to be a wealthy Chicago banker, had made every cent of his money by scamming people. He sent out bundles of printed tickets to business owners across the country with a letter attached stating that they had been personally selected as one of the few lucky establishments to be included in this once-in-a-lifetime opportunity. It was very simple; business owners would sell the tickets to their patrons for an inflated price, then they would keep a percentage of the profits for themselves and send the rest of the money back to the lottery company, which was Gourdain himself. The tickets were supposed to be for a lottery to win a jackpot of money. No one ever suspected that there was never any drawing—they just assumed that they had not won. Gourdain made what would equal millions of dollars in today's money simply by having people hand money to him, but it eventually caught up with him.

Gourdain had been arrested in New York again for the same lottery scam. He continued his crazy antics during this trial. The court foolishly gave Gourdain a stack of blank summons so that he could send them out himself. Gourdain didn't send them to people involved in the case. Instead, he sent hundreds of them to celebrities, elected officials and even one to the Czar of Russia.

On the day of his trial, many of the summoned showed up one by one very confused. The court apologized to all and sent everyone home. Louis was convicted of his crimes and remanded to the Government Hospital for the Insane in Washington, D.C., by the court. He would not make headline news again for a few years until 1908, when he surfaced in London after escaping the hospital in D.C.

Gourdain was on a roll again; he was claiming that he was part of a secret society that had begun in 1903 in Chicago. The society's mission was to overthrow the United States government and make it a monarchy in which his friend "Helen of New York" would be queen. He said a great war was going to come, as there were sects of the secret society in every state waiting for a signal to take over. After his mad rantings made the front page of a paper in Washington, D.C., officials were hot on his trail. Gourdain went into hiding and was not heard from again until May of 1913, when Chicago government officials received word that he had died in London.

Gourdain only spent a little time inside Old Joliet, but it seems the place got under his skin to the point where it literally drove him crazy. Gourdain is a great candidate for being one of the dark shadows that has been seen roaming about the prison grounds. Maybe Louis Gourdain got what he wished for when he passed from this world into the next—and you know what they say about that.

LEOPOLD AND LOEB

It was called the crime of the century. Fourteen-year-old Bobby Franks, the son of a wealthy Chicago watchmaker, went missing from a Chicago suburb after school in the spring of 1924. His body was found near Wolf Lake in Hammond, Indiana, the next day. The community was shocked and shaken. This type of thing, which is sadly more common today, did not happen back then. Who in the world would do such a thing to an innocent young boy? The answer to this question came through a simple pair of eyeglasses found near the body. The hinges on the glasses were unique and thus traceable. They were sold to only three people in the Chicago area. One of them was nineteen-year-old Nathan Leopold, the son of a wealthy local transport and freight mogul from Germany. When questioned about the eyeglasses, Leopold said that he must have dropped them during a birdwatching trip he had made the week before.

The story that unfolded in the weeks after the discovery of the eyeglasses was one that is still hard to believe today. Leopold, along with his friend and schoolmate Richard Loeb, who was eighteen, had kidnapped and murdered Bobby Franks in an attempt to commit the perfect murder. Loeb was the son of a wealthy Chicago family as well. All three boys were from the same neighborhood. Bobby was a distant cousin to Loeb and had even visited the Leopold home several times to play tennis. Leopold and Loeb, as they were later most famously known, were egoists who had grown up in wealth and privilege. Richard Loeb was highly intelligent, and Leopold was a handsome, charismatic young man. They formed a friendship in which their differences complemented each other well—too well. Together, they believed they had become untouchable.

After their arrest, they revealed that, in the year before the murder, they had committed a series of petty crimes of vandalism and thievery. Getting away without detection was a powerful drug, and it fueled them to commit crimes that were a little more dangerous each time. They eventually progressed to burglarizing fraternity houses and setting things on fire. Still, no one noticed or had any clue what these young men were up to. They then spent several months planning what they called "the perfect murder." On the afternoon of May 24, 1924, the pair, ready to put their plan into action, came across Bobby Franks as he was walking home from school. They pulled over and offered him a ride. At first, Bobby declined the ride, as he was only a few blocks from his home. They finally convinced him to get into the car after telling him there was something they wanted to talk to him about. What happened next would be disputed by both Leopold and Loeb. Each gave basically the same account of what happened in the car between the pickup point and where they dumped the body, but there was one main difference. Each claimed that he was the driver and that the other had murdered the boy in the back seat.

By the time the duo arrived back at home from their horrible deed, word had already spread that Bobby was missing. The plan they had concocted included making the Franks family believe their son had been kidnapped and then successfully extorting a large ransom from them. Leopold made a call to the Frankses' home that night and told Bobby's mother that he had her son and that instructions would follow on how to pay the ransom. A typed note arrived at the Franks home the next morning, accompanied shortly by a second call from Leopold in which he told the family where to find the next set of directions. The plan started to go south at this point, as the Franks family member who took the call did not write down the destination address correctly. A short time later, Bobby's body was discovered, and the ransom attempt was exposed as being fake. A massive investigation was launched using the press and offers of rewards for any information regarding the murder. Leopold was so bold as to talk to the press and tell them how he thought he would have committed the crime had he done it.

On May 29, eight days after the murder, both Leopold and Loeb were brought in by police for formal questioning. Loeb cracked first and confessed. Leopold followed after he was told of his partner's confession. Both adamantly blamed the other for the actual murder. Legendary Chicago lawyer Clarence Darrow was called in by the families. He had agreed to defend the murdering pair simply because of his staunch opposition to capital punishment. Darrow would be key in keeping them from being executed but knew that they would never be acquitted. They would both plead guilty, and a thirty-two-day-long sentencing hearing brought out all the dirty details. Darrow claimed that the boys' privileged lifestyles and absence of parental guidance are what led them to becoming the troubled, uncaring individuals that committed this crime. Loeb also testified that he was molested by a former governess. Darrow gave a three-day-long closing argument and was successful in saving them both from the electric chair. Their fate was life in Joliet Prison.

Nathan Leopold and Richard Loeb both began their prison stays at Old Joliet on September 12, 1924. Their arrival at the prison was as sensational as the rest of their case. On their ride to the prison, the car they were riding in was traveling at a high speed and being followed by press. The car briefly lost control at one point and careened off the road, almost turning over. The driver managed to regain control and delivered them, though shaken up, in one piece.

Armed guards with guns drawn lined both sides of the front entrance as Leopold and Loeb were rushed inside and out of public sight for good. The media was present but were told by Leopold that they were instructed not to talk. They were now in custody of the Joliet Penitentiary and would live just as all the other prisoners did. Their first night was spent in solitary cells, the same as all new prisoners. Their first day was filled with inmate processing procedures and learning the ropes. The second day, they rose like the rest of the prisoners and began the routine of prison life. Loeb was assigned to the chairmaking factory, and Leopold was assigned to the rattan department. They were placed in opposite cellblocks to assure there was no contact between the two. Leopold was transferred to the brand-new Stateville facility after it was opened in 1925. Loeb stayed at the old prison for a longer period because Warden Hill said they needed to keep them as far from each other as possible. The boys had opposing experiences inside the prisons.

Eight months into his sentence, "Dickie" Loeb started becoming delusional and violent. At first, the guards thought he was pretending in order to get out of jail and into the hospital, but eventually, they realized there was something truly wrong with him. Usually an almost model prisoner, he started screaming at the guards and throwing things about. Doctors at the prison hospital diagnosed him with the measles. He spent thirty-six hours strapped to a bed, running a high fever, thrashing about and calling for someone named Buddy. It was reported by an unnamed friend of the family that Buddy was a nickname for the girl he dated before his arrest, but the similarity between Buddy and Bobby, especially when being vocalized under the stressful conditions of severe illness, is too close not to wonder if his cries for his girlfriend were mistaken and actually a desperate cry of regret. Confinement within the walls of a prison tends to make people face their demons. Was Loeb calling out for the young boy whose life he had taken, or was he possibly seeing Bobby Franks as other murderers have seen their victims inside the limestone Joliet walls?

Thirteen years later, in January 1938, Richard Loeb was killed by fellow inmate James Day. Day later claimed that the murder weapon, a straight razor, belonged to Loeb and that the bathroom the incident occurred in was Loeb's private bathroom to which he had the only key. Day testified that Loeb had invited him to the bathroom that morning to settle their differences. After arriving, Day rebuked sexual advances from Loeb to which Loeb threatened him with the razor if he did not cooperate. Day lunged for Loeb and was able to overcome him and take the razor. Releasing the pent-up anger that he had been building up for some time against Loeb, Day slashed him more than fifty times. Loeb was rushed to the prison hospital but was in critical condition. His family called in the best doctors from the University of Chicago, but despite all their efforts, Richard Loeb died two hours later, at 3:05 p.m.

Day was tried and acquitted for Loeb's murder. During the trial, Day described Loeb as a seasoned prisoner who preyed on the incoming new and younger inmates. The confrontation in the bathroom was the culmination of a long string of similar incidents between the two, with Loeb always the aggressor. Prison administration denied the accusations that Loeb had privileges above and beyond what others were afforded. However, five prisoners testified in support of Day's testimony. They had all had similar problems with Loeb, and they said that Loeb was a known predator.

Nathan Leopold had his own stint in the prison hospital some years later. After Loeb's death, he became a model prisoner and was instrumental in helping Stateville Prison form and update some of its educational programs and resources. He also volunteered in the prison hospital. In 1946, he joined a research project that allowed doctors to inject him with the live malaria virus and then test different treatments on him. His efforts eventually helped him be paroled in 1958. Nathan Leopold immediately moved to Puerto Rico on his release and spent the rest of his life teaching at a university there. He was married in 1961 and published a book on ornithology before dying of a heart attack in 1971.

Nathan Leopold lived out his life quietly. He used his life in prison to help others, give back and reflect on the horrible thing that he had done. Loeb, on the other hand, went out with a sensational bang. He never really seemed to be very remorseful for what he had done. Maybe if he had had more time, remorse would have come with age, but we will never know. Loeb was quoted as saying how much he disliked the old prison and how terrible the conditions there were. What more of a perfect punishment for the perfect crime than to be stuck for eternity in the place you hated most. Loeb could still be walking the halls of Old Joliet, serving a sentence that was not long enough in life.

Adolf Luetgert

Chicago Sausage King

Adolf Luetgert was well known in the latter part of the 1800s as Chicago's sausage king. He was later known worldwide as the man who ground his wife into sausage. He was sentenced to life in Old Joliet for the murder, and the sensation it caused around the world was legendary. The trial was the stage for introducing new methods of science that police were beginning to use in murder investigations. It was also one of the first times that a man was convicted of murder without there being a dead body to even prove the death of the victim. Adolf was found dead in his cell in Old Joliet after serving only a year and a half. He staunchly claimed his innocence but to no avail—very few believed him.

Born in Gutersloh, Germany, Adolph Ludwig Luetgert was one of ten siblings. His father was a tanner, and as a young man, Adolph apprenticed in the same industry. A few years later, he began traveling around Germany, settling for small periods of time where he could find work. At nineteen years of age, he went to London, only to leave six months later when he was not able to find work. In 1866, he immigrated to New York, as was the trend for young men who were looking to make their way in life at the time. He left New York a few months after arriving to join a friend and his brother in Quincy, Illinois, where he again only stayed for a few months before moving to Chicago to work at a tannery. He married his first wife, Caroline, in 1872, and they had two children. Only one survived, his son Arnold. Two months after Caroline's death, he married his second wife, Louisa, with whom he had four more children; only two of their sons survived.

Adolf worked in the tanning industry, saving as much money as he could. By 1879, he had saved $4,000 and bought a saloon. The business did well, and the couple was able to save most of their profits by living frugally above the saloon in small rooms. They were soon in the position to make their move to a newer, better business venture, when the opportunity arose for them to buy a meat route. The saloon was sold, and the small family moved above the local market. Adolf then went to work selling meat from a cart, door to door to friends and locals. Their newest venture proved to be even more profitable than the saloon. As his meat route grew steadily, Adolf began making sausages from his home country in the back rooms of the market and selling them alongside the meat. The sausage was a huge hit, and the little business grew rapidly with the expansion of a few different types of sausages. By 1891, the Luetgerts had managed to save $80,000, and the business was thriving. They built a factory and a beautiful house next to it. Until this point, the story is almost a fairy tale. Through hard work and sparse living, a couple who had come to this country for a better life had not only made it but thrived. It was the American dream.

Unfortunately, this is also the point at which their story turns ugly. Adolf and Louisa had very different ideas of how they should move forward with growing their business. Their lifestyles began to go in opposite directions as well. He wanted to invest their entire savings into his grand vision of a massive six-story building that would be able to produce sausage and ship it around the world, and she wanted to invest half the money into the sausage plant and half into something else to secure their future. He eventually won, and the huge factory was built.

In 1893, the year the world's fair was in Chicago, the A.L. Luetgert Sausage Works made $75,000 (the 2020 equivalent is $2.1 million). That's a lot of sausage. It was also a tremendous amount of money back then. The sausage company continued to prosper, as the sausages were in high demand across the country. Louisa continued down her path of working hard and living frugally. She worried constantly that, at any moment, hard times could hit and that they would lose everything, as they didn't have much to fall back on. She worried not only for herself but for the thriving little community that had been built around the sausage factory. Their employees had, over time, built small houses within a mile of the factory, and many had come to depend on it for their livelihoods.

Adolf was hailed as the sausage king of Chicago, but with the success, he seemed to go in the exact opposite direction of his wife of twenty years. He was spending less time in the factory and home as he spent more time with the new friends who had come with the money. Eventually, those friends included women with whom he carried out affairs.

Louisa was very unhappy with the way things were going; she berated and belittled Adolf for what she saw as irresponsible behavior. As time went on and the behavior got worse, so did the fighting. It got so out of hand that Louisa's family and friends were concerned for her safety. Adolf was a hulking man with a murderous temper and was known to get physical with her. Louisa was a strong woman but was physically small. Eventually, Adolf fixed a room for himself to sleep in at his factory, and from then on, he was only ever seen at the family home at mealtimes.

Mary Siemering entered the household sometime in the year before Louisa's disappearance. She was Louisa's distant cousin and was brought in as a housemaid, much to Louisa's dismay. Adolf was enamored with the young woman and was open in his admiration for her. This became a big arguing point for Adolf and Louisa; she wanted Mary out of her house, and Adolf refused, telling Louisa that if she should put Mary out he would take her in with him at the factory. The last thing Louisa needed was the embarrassment of her husband taking up with the maid in the factory for all to see, so she acquiesced, and Mary stayed.

In the spring of 1897, the factory shut down in preparation for a massive renovation Adolf had planned. Louisa was against these new plans and did not miss a chance to tell Adolf. She nagged at him to set aside the expansion plans and to be content with the comfortable life they led. In April of that year, one of their investors foreclosed on a $30,000 mortgage. The firm, Forman Brothers, agreed with Louisa that the plans for the sausage factory were too grandiose and farfetched to be possible. The plans for the expansion were dropped as, one by one, the other investors followed suit and dropped out as well.

The couple's arguments grew more frequent and violent. Louisa blamed Adolf for their ruin. She never missed a chance to remind him that, had he listened to her, they would not have been in this position. She had worked hard for many years next to this man, helping him build the successful company that should have kept them comfortable for the rest of their lives. Instead, at an advanced age, they were back at square one with nothing. By the end of April, with no income and all avenues exhausted, the bank notes were piling up. At any moment, the bank was going to come and take everything they had built.

The last time anyone saw Louisa Luetgert was May 1, 1897. The next day, May 2, Adolf told his sons that their mother had gone to visit her sister the night before and had not returned. Louisa's brother, Deidrich Dicknesse, called at the Luetgert home three days later. When he arrived, not only did he find that his sister had been missing for a few days but that Adolf, totally aloof and indifferent, had not informed authorities of her disappearance. Dicknesse went to the authorities, and when they interviewed Adolf, he told them that she had run off with another man. As the police began to investigate, they learned that Adolf had been seen going into the factory with Louisa by a night watchman who was on duty at the factory on the night of May 1 around 10:30 p.m. The watchman told investigators that Adolf had given him an errand to run that evening and had then told him to take the rest of the night off. Investigators had also located bills that showed Adolf had purchased arsenic and potash the day before Louisa was last seen. Neighbors reported that they had seen smoke coming from the closed-down factory later that night and that it continued until early morning. All of the evidence pointed to Adolf killing Louisa in the factory that night. The police finally went in to search the factory. They found human residue among burned spoiled sausages in the furnace. In a large vat inside the factory, they found human bone fragments and two gold rings, one of which had the initials "L.L." engraved on the inside. The bone was later identified by a forensic anthropologist as being fragments from the toe, foot, rib and skull of a human female. The rings were identified as Louisa's wedding rings.

Adolf was arrested on May 18 and was indicted by a grand jury shortly after; however, he still proclaimed his innocence. The murder of Louisa and the trial of her husband was one of the first cases of its kind. It was highly publicized in newspaper headlines across the country. People were horrified but fascinated by the grisly details emerging about the case. When preparing for the trial in the beginning of August 1897, the prosecution obtained a corpse and boiled it in the same vat that they suspected had been used to do the very same to Louisa Luetgert. After boiling the body in caustic potash for two hours, all the flesh and most of the bones were reduced to liquid, leaving only the larger bones intact.

The first trial began in the latter part of August 1897. The defense claimed that they, too, had conducted the same boiling experiment but had totally different results. Their corpse did not disintegrate at all, and the prosecution's theory that Adolf had killed Louisa, boiled her body and then tried to destroy any remains in the furnace did not hold. They emphatically denied that a murder had even occurred and said that Mrs. Luetgert had simply left of her own free will on the night of May 1 due to her despondency over the impending demise of their lives. They went as far as to suggest that Louisa had committed suicide.

Strangely enough, sightings of Mrs. Luetgert after the alleged murder date popped up all over the country. She was reported as being seen in twelve different states; one of them was New York, where she was supposedly boarding a ship for England. None of the sightings ever amounted to anything. After Adolf's conviction, there was only one sighting that claimed Louisa was alive and well. An eighty-two-year-old woman came into the police department claiming that she could produce Louisa Luetgert in the flesh. She just needed them to give her some money first. The old woman was thanked kindly and sent on her way.

Through the entire proceedings of the first trial, Adolf was described as looking confident that he would be found innocent of all charges. Concluding in October, the trial ended with a hung jury—three against conviction and nine for. After thirty-six hours of deliberation, the jury could still not vote unanimously, so the judge dismissed them. A little over a month later, a second trial was called. This time, the prosecution upped its game. The clincher this time was a forensic anthropologist from the Chicago History Museum. On the stand, he gave expert testimony that the bone fragments found in the furnace were indeed human and female. Witnesses also took the stand to attest to the violent history of the Luetgerts' fighting. Several of them told of how Adolf often talked of how much he hated his wife and that he wanted to "crush" her. This trial lasted about six weeks. Adolf also took the stand to tell his story from his own lips. He made outrageous claims while on the stand that he was being set up by the government, which wanted to take his money. In the end, his testimony did him more harm than good. It only took the jury about five minutes to deliberate before agreeing he was guilty. On February 9, 1898, Adolf Luetgert was sentenced to life in prison for the murder of his wife, Louisa Luetgert, and he was remanded to the Old Joliet Penitentiary. He was given life in prison instead of the death penalty because the jury felt it was the harsher punishment.

His stay in Old Joliet was a tormented one. Although he continued to proclaim his innocence, the evidence was just too overwhelming for most to believe him. His lawyer, Lawrence Harmon, who had been his staunch advocate throughout the second trial, continued to try to prove his innocence. Both still claimed Louisa was somewhere out there, hiding in the world. Harmon spent thousands of his own money trying to find Louisa, and he tirelessly looked for those willing to support Adolf's mounting legal expenses.

Prison officials were happy to have the man who grew such a successful production business from the ground up. They put him to work in their meat department and had plans to have him start making sausages. Meanwhile, Adolf did not adapt to prison life well. The stress of the murder and subsequent trial was believed to have driven him literally mad. In the last months of his life, Adolf was said to have been mentally declining as well. He was reported as displaying bizarre behavior and walking around babbling to himself in the prison yard. Among those babbles were his repeated claims that Louisa, his dead, murdered wife, visited him in his prison cell at night. All night long, she would sit with him, scolding him relentlessly about his having lost everything and letting him know she would be there to haunt him for the rest of his days for taking her life. This time, there was no way for him to escape it. He was locked inside a tiny cell for ten hours a night, forced to listen to the very voice he tried to extinguish. This is kind of condemning when you consider he claimed to believe she was out there somewhere, playing a great trick on everyone.

His prison stay only lasted eighteen months. His health was on a steady decline from the moment he walked through Joliet's iron bars. Over the years, some of the prisoners who came from a wealthier lifestyle and were used to a much higher-quality food regimen had a difficult time adjusting to the plain, coarse prison food. Their bodies just could not adapt, and thus, severe physical ailments resulted. On the morning of July 7, 1899, shortly after he had gotten his breakfast, Adolf Luetgert was found dead on the floor of his cell. An autopsy later revealed heart disease as the reason for his death. Today, we know that stress and a fatty diet are the two main things that cause a plethora of heart problems. Adolf had plenty of both. Just before his death, he had learned that his brother-in-law had won custody of his young sons after a long court battle. Adolf was infuriated by this, and they said his heart was already in bad shape. The added stress simply stopped his heart for good.

Adolf Luetgert's wake and funeral were just as bizarre and gruesome as the rest of his story. Hundreds came to the wake out of morbid curiosity to see the man who had ground his wife up in his factory and sold her as sausage. The rumor mill, as usual, had run rampant, making sausage quite unpopular in the Chicago area after the findings at the Leutgert factory, even though no sausage had been made during the time of Louisa's murder. Members of the Luetgert family were there, including Adolf's oldest son, Arnold. Louisa's family and sons were not present. A single flower arrangement in the shape of a pillow rested at the head of the coffin. Made of crimson roses and white carnations, the flowers bore a simple inscription across the top: OUR FATHER'S WORDS: "I AM INNOCENT."

Adolf's lawyer, Harmon, was one of the last to show up at the wake. The crowd was so big that there was no room inside, and people were spilling out the door and into the streets; most of them were spectators who were just trying to catch a glimpse of the infamous murderer. Before the services started, Harmon took a noted stance in front of Adolf's still form in the coffin. As hundreds of mourners, including the Luetgert family, looked on, stunned, Harmon shouted for Louisa Luetgert to make an appearance: "I call upon Louisa Luetgert, the missing woman, for whom he suffered without ever uttering an unkind word regarding her, to come forth and remove the unmerited stain from the name of the father of her innocent children." He then gave an eye-to-eye stare to many of those in the room in order to magnify the words he had just spoken. Harmon went on to try to find Louisa for a few years after Adolf died. He was eventually institutionalized and died in an asylum some years later.

For many years after the trial, the spirit of Louisa was spotted wandering around in the family home next to the sausage plant in Chicago. The house sat vacant for many years. No one wanted to live where a vengeful spirit was said to roam. When enough time had passed, the grisly crime faded from people's minds. Families rented the home but were said to never have stayed very long. In 1907, the home was moved from its original location at 207 Hermitage Avenue to a lot on Diversey Street near Paulina Avenue. It was renovated and sold. No other Louisa sightings were ever reported again.

5

TELEVISION AND MOVIES

The already famous prison graduated to celebrity status in 1980 with the release of the movie *The Blues Brothers*, which was written by and starred John Belushi as Joliet Jake Blues and Dan Akroyd as his brother, Elwood Blues. The opening scene of the movie shows Joliet Jake being released from prison. The walk from his cell to the sally port he exits from was all filmed at Old Joliet. In the film, Jake finds his brother Elwood waiting for him just outside the prison in an old beat-up cop car, and hilarity ensues.

Legendary shenanigans happened throughout the filming of the movie. Years later, Dan Akroyd revealed that an allowance for cocaine was included in the movie's budget to keep the actors and crew awake during the night shoots. Apparently, this did not work, as they discovered after Belushi disappeared during one of the night shoots. Dan Akroyd found him in a house a short distance away; he had wandered in randomly and asked the occupants for a sandwich and glass of milk. After his request was fulfilled, he promptly passed out on their sofa, where Akroyd found him.

At the time of filming, Old Joliet was still a fully functional prison. A helicopter was used to shoot some overhead scenes for the movie. On one occasion, prison guards who did not know this shot at the helicopter, as they thought it was someone spying on the prison. *The Blues Brothers* was Old Joliet's most famous appearance, but it was not its first.

A documentary on life inside Joliet Penitentiary was filmed in 1914, during the administration of Warden Edmund M. Allen. The film was originally titled *Life in Joliet Penitentiary* and was also later referred to as *The Modern Prison*. Shot as an educational film, the documentary shows the daily

"THE BLUES BROTHERS"   2127-22   Jake and Elwood Blues (JOHN BELUSHI and DAN AYKROYD) perform in prison.

John Belushi and Dan Akroyd onstage during the filming of *The Blues Brothers. Courtesy of the Joliet Area Historical Museum.*

routine of a prisoner in the Old Joliet Penitentiary during the early twentieth century, a time when the facility was well known as a model prison. The film details an inmate's life at Joliet, from his incarceration to his discharge. Scenes from the film also showed the interior and exterior workings of the prison's manufacturing shops, kitchen, dining room and chapel services and a tour of the cell houses.

The prison has been referred to in too many television series, films, songs and other forms of art to count. Memphis Minnie recorded a song titled "Joliet Bound" with Kansas Joe McCoy in 1932. In 1963, Bob Dylan wrote "Percy's Song" for his third album. Joan Baez performed the song in the documentary of Dylan's 1965 England tour, but the song was not released until 1985 on his album *Biograph*. The song was written from the point of view of the narrating character whose friend was driving a car involved in a fatal car crash. In the song, the driver of the car is convicted of manslaughter, for which he received a ninety-nine-year sentence in Joliet Prison. The narrator asks the sentencing judge to lighten his friend's harsh sentence, but the judge refuses.

In 2005, the movie *Derailed*, starring Jennifer Aniston and Clive Owens, filmed multiple scenes at the Joliet prison. Later that year, Fox filmed the first season of its mega hit *Prison Break* there. The filming continued into 2006, with Old Joliet playing the part of Fox River Penitentiary. The show's creators searched everywhere for a location. When they finally found the Joliet prison, they were thrilled. Not only was the building beautiful and impressive, but it had been closed for three years and needed almost no alterations to complete the scenes that were needed. The naturally dark, ominous and depressing atmosphere of the prison helped actor Wentworth Miller connect with his character on set. He said if he needed inspiration, he needed to only look up at the limestone walls around him and imagine what life had been like locked inside the claustrophobic cells for years on end.

On the show, Miller's character, Michael Scofield, who had blueprints of the prison tattooed on his body, robbed a bank in order to be thrown into the Fox River Penitentiary, where his brother was serving time for a crime he swore he did not do. Scofield's goal was to break out of Fox River, also known as Old Joliet, with his brother, Lincoln Burrows (played by actor Dominique

The Chicago Bluesmobile is for rent for your party or event! *Photograph by Brian Scanlan. Courtesy of thechicagobluesmobile@gmail.com.*

Purcell). Burrows was involved in a plot hatched by the vice president, and the murdered man he was serving time for was the vice president's brother. Amaury Nelasco, who plays Michael Scofield's cellmate in the series, said that he looked forward to leaving the prison and its disturbing vibe behind at night. "The minute you walk in, you feel this energy and the cloud of all the spirits that are probably going by. The prison is a character in itself. It's there. You have to acknowledge it." The first of five seasons of *Prison Break* was shot on the Old Joliet Prison site. The rest was mostly filmed on soundstages and locations in Chicago. The five seasons ended the show's original run on Fox in 2017, but it has had recent resurgence in popularity due to the series being available through online streaming services.

The old prison was most recently featured on the popular entertainment show *Ghost Adventures*. The ghost-hunting crew filmed a one-hour special on the prison for its limited series "Serial Killer Spirits." The episode featured local and prison photographer Rob Johnson. Rob shared his personal experiences as he walked through the prison with the crew. The *Ghost Adventures* crew encountered some spooky happenings inside the prison and wondered if they had captured the spirit of John Wayne Gacy, who spent a brief time at the Joliet facility. The prison's appearance in pop culture media has boosted tourism in Joliet. Visitors come in from all over the world to see the Joliet Jakes Cell or where Linc Burrows shot basketball.

6

THE MURDER OF THE WARDEN'S WIFE

At the beginning of 1915, everything was going fantastically well at Joliet Prison. The warden and the prison itself were being praised for being one of the top-rated penal institutes in the country. Warden Edmund Allen was said to have turned the prison around almost overnight when he took the position. He was a man with modern ideas about prison reform and believed that all men had it within them to change their ways with a little care and guidance. Odette Allen was Edmund's wife. She was his equal in advocating for the men he had been put in charge of. She was not only exceptionally beautiful, but she was said to be the epitome of kindness. A shining beacon of light in the dark prison, they called her the angel of Joliet. Her death on the prison's grounds still echoes sadness through the limestone walls, 105 years later.

Edmund M. Allen was born and raised in Joliet, Illinois. His father served as warden of Joliet Prison in its very early years, so it was no surprise to anyone when Edmund, or Ned as he was called by friends and family, followed in his father's footsteps in his career choice. Politically, Ned was his father's opposite. Where the senior Allen was all about old-school strict discipline, Ned was well known as a radical modernist.

Edmund married his first wife, Isabel, in 1894 and had two children with her: John in 1896 and Katherine in 1897. Sadly, Isabel died in May 1903 from pneumonia and exhaustion. A few years later, at an event in Chicago, Edmund met Odette Bordeaux, a divorced singer with the Merry Widow

Company based out of her hometown of New Orleans. The romance that developed between the two was a whirlwind. They were married quietly in April 1909, and Odette left the stage life behind for her new hometown of Joliet, Illinois. At the time, Edmund was a police magistrate and was already well known for his modernist views. He was elected mayor of Joliet in 1911 and held the position until 1913, when he was appointed warden of the Illinois State Penitentiary at Joliet.

The turn of the century saw the banishment of the prison's harsher ways. The striped uniforms were gone, and the strict no-talking rule was partially lifted. Warden Allen's predecessor, E.J. Murphy, had been slowly making some of the changes that prison reform was bringing. When Allen took over in 1913, he wasted no time in implementing the radical ideas he believed in. Overnight, harsh policies were overturned and more liberal ones put in place, allowing more freedom in the daily life of the prisoners. To his core, Allen believed that all men had it in them to change. With a little care and guidance, they could all become better men, even if it was just inside the prison. His ideas brought hope to the men inside the prison, something that the prison's previous hard ways had beat out of them.

He established what was called the Honor System in which prisoners who were serving time could earn privileges, better work assignments and liberties for good behavior. The highest honor was to be chosen by the warden himself to serve as house staff to his family. The warden's quarters were on the second floor of the administration building. Allen lived here with Odette and his two children. It may seem strange to some that he would want his very beautiful wife anywhere near the hardened, crass men who were the occupants of the prison, but Ned believed her presence among the men could bring out the most basic humanity in them. Everyone, even hardened criminals, had a mom, and that is exactly how the inmates saw her—she was the little mama at the Big Sur.

The Allens were adored by the inmates. It is easy to see why when you read about the care and concern they showed to everyone at the prison. Warden Allen affectionately called the inmates at Joliet "My Boys" and treated them with kindness and understanding. Odette was equally active in the care of the men at the prison. Her connections in the entertainment world brought some of the country's top acts there to give complimentary performances, and sometimes, she would sing for them herself. The couple was clearly dedicated to bettering the men's lives.

A series of fires broke out in the prison outbuildings in the beginning of January 1914. The first two were snuffed out shortly after they started, and they caused no major damage. Officials knew that it was arson but had no idea who had started them. The third fire broke out in the shop where furniture was made. By the time this blaze was spotted, it had already engulfed a good part of the building. The prison's fire department and Joliet's fire department were able to put the fire out. In the process, the guilty inmate was discovered and thrown in solitary. Afterward, the papers carried the story of how all the convicts who were able pulled together to help distinguish the fire. Because of the fire, multiple exits had been opened, but not one escape attempt was made. Allen was a proud father, boasting that his boys had come together to vanquish the fire and capture the bad guy. His system was not only working but excelling. No one seemed to want to mention that the incident, which had done extensive damage to the prison shop, was created by an inmate in that same system.

The next winter, Allen's right-hand man, Deputy Warden Walsh, became severely ill before eventually passing in the late spring. After his death, Warden Allen appealed to the governor for some time off. He was exhausted from the last months of handling a heavy workload while watching his friend slowly die. He was granted a week of leave that he planned to spend at the hot springs in West Baden, Indiana, with Odette to rest, relax and regroup. The couple had spent two years tirelessly attending to and advocating for the prison. The vacation was a much-needed respite that they were both looking forward to. The warden left on Saturday, June 19. Odette was originally supposed to go with him but had decided to wait until the next day to join her husband. They were to attend a charity event during their stay in Baden, and the dress she had commissioned for the event was not finished. She told Ned she would join him Sunday, after the dress was delivered to her. However, Odette would never leave the prison.

Very early on Sunday morning (June 20, 1915), Mrs. Allen's service button was ringing loudly and continuously, as if someone was frantically pushing it. Curious as to why the call had not been answered by her personal servant, Joe, another house servant went to find him. It was then that they smelled the smoke. The fire alarm was pulled, and within minutes, the prison's firefighters arrived at the scene. It took them a few minutes to determine the smoke was coming from inside the warden's quarters. Once they forced their way through the main door, they could clearly see that it was coming from inside Mrs. Allen's bedroom on the second floor. The door had been locked from the inside and had to be forced down as well. When they finally made it through, the bed was engulfed in flames, and the room filled with smoke. The visibility was close to none, causing much confusion. Everyone was asking where Mrs. Allen was. One of the men reported that she was safe; he said he had seen her going up the stairs to the third floor. It was not until they were able to extinguish the fire and clear some of the smoke that they noticed her body. Odette Allen lay on the floor, a halo of blood around her head, burnt beyond recognition.

After examining the scene and the body, it was determined that Odette had been hit with a blunt object on her right temple, hard enough to fracture her skull. The blow itself did not kill her, but it rendered her unconscious. Smoke inhalation was the final cause of death, and it was suspected the object used to strike her was a metal water pitcher. Wood alcohol that was kept in a ceramic jug in the room was used to soak the bedding and the body before they were set on fire. Pieces of the broken jug were found scattered throughout the scene.

Twelve inmates who had access to the Allen family's living quarters were immediately sequestered in solitary. The fire and the chaos it caused happened while the inmates were having breakfast that morning. The dining hall was directly behind where the warden's quarters were. It was obvious to all of them that something was very wrong. The first men on the scene were inmates who worked in the prison's fire department. It did not take long for word to make it down the grapevine, spreading the news to the prison population. Their angel was dead, violently murdered by one of their own, and the main suspect was Mrs. Allen's personal houseman, "Chicken" Joe Campbell. By lunchtime, the inmates were in a fury, and an uprising had begun in the dining hall. Inmates began throwing chairs and arming themselves with whatever they could get their hands on. The mob was calling for Campbell's head, and there were shouts of "We'll tear him to pieces!" As the raging prisoners started to move toward the door to make good on their threats, they were met by one hundred guards armed with clubs. The guards went in, cracked some heads and had them under control in fifteen minutes. Warden Allen then shut down the entire prison, locking down all inmates until the situation could be investigated and tempers cooled. The prisoners were then further subdued by a plea from Warden Allen for them to remain calm and to let officials do their job in securing justice for his wife. He swore to them that the man who had done the crime would be found and held accountable, but he said that he wanted to make sure, beyond a doubt, that they had the right man.

Joe Campbell was suspect number one. He was personally selected by Odette to be her houseman. Campbell was serving a sentence in Joliet for killing a man in Chicago in 1913. Of all the house servants, Joe had the most access to the Allens' home, and he was the last person to see her alive. Joe's story was that he had started his day early, at 6:00 a.m., when he was summoned by Mrs. Allen to fetch her newspapers. Joe said he fetched the papers and poured her a pitcher of ice water. She then told him that she was going back to bed and asked him to tell the barber that she wanted her hair washed later that morning. The last Joe saw of her, she had gone back to bed and left the door unlocked so that he could take her dog out for a walk. It was when he returned from walking the dog that he saw smoke and the men trying to break down the door to the bedroom.

Warden Allen received the horrific news via telephone that morning. He was crushed. He later told those around him that he had a bad feeling that he should not have left her alone. The day before, he had purchased a $3,000 ring that was a matching mate to one he had previously bought for her, and he had made plans to give it to her that night. Warden Allen returned to Joliet immediately after receiving the call. It had been explained to him on the phone that Odette had been severely injured, but officers did not want to tell him that she had died over the phone. He did not learn of her death until he arrived home.

Warden Allen privately interviewed each of the eleven men who were being held as possible suspects in his office. Joe Campbell had to be surrounded and completely covered by guards as they moved him from solitary confinement to the warden's office. Warden Allen was hoping that a personal appeal to the men would elicit a confession or at least some information from the one or ones who were guilty, but no such admission ever came forth.

Everyone who knew Odette was devastated by the news. She was loved not only by the inmates but by the people of Joliet. A letter written and signed by the inmates and sent to Warden Allen shows the depth of the sadness the whole prison felt.

> *At this hour of deepest grief, we send you this message of our love and sympathy. Caesar had his Brutus, Rome its Nero and Jesus the Just his Judas. Yet, the remnants of his disciples remained steadfast, and true treachery and betrayal were in vain. His work endures. So, in spite of the dreadful blow which has fallen upon us, the work of yourself and your wife must go on.*
>
> *Let us all, you and us, take new hope and, over the grave of her who poured out her love for us, join hands and resolve to finish the work which you have begun.*
>
> *The eyes of the world are upon us, and we must succeed. We may each and all of us pledge ourselves to wipe out the tragic stain by making your*

work here a success. The hour has struck, and we cannot retreat. Come back to us, and we will build together a real honor system as a fitting memorial to your dear departed wife that will be more lasting and enduring than marble or bronze. We will build men in whom honor is not dead and will not die.

Our hearts are heavy with grief, and our eyes are wet with tears because of this sad tragedy.

For your wife and our friend, Odette Allen, words cannot express our thoughts nor speech contain our love.

—Your Boys

Joe was indicted by the grand jury five days after the murder. The testimony that came out during the inquest and trial about his bizarre behavior during the time of the fire was very condemning. It was not the behavior of an innocent man. Two men who were also house staff members gave identical accounts of seeing Joe leave the warden's quarters with the dog. They said he glanced backward at the building several times as he walked across the lawn. One observing this behavior may have reached the conclusion that he was watching for something he knew was about to happen. The volunteer firemen who were on the scene all gave the same accounts of Joe having interfered with their efforts to get into the bedroom and extinguish the fire. It was said he went as far as to put a table and bureau behind one of the doorways. The firemen also testified that someone had turned the water off twice while they were putting the fire out.

The evidence that was mounting against Joe was mostly circumstantial. What tipped the scales against him was his confession that he had stolen Odette's purse and hidden it in a closet outside the bedroom. Joe later said that the confession was coerced out of him due to exhaustion from the days of questioning by police and officials. The purse, according to Warden Allen, held his wife's jewelry and one hundred dollars in cash. He said she kept it under her pillow at night for safe keeping. Police found the purse inside a closet that was used for linen storage; it was found wrapped in a pillow cover and hidden behind some blankets. The pillow cover had fresh blood on it, and they also found a piece of bloodstained collar hidden in Joe's cell when they searched it. When asked about the blood, Joe told them it was his from cutting himself shaving, but there was no wound found on him.

Other testimony given said that Joe and one other housemate were seen changing their clothing just after the fire had been put out. It was not looking good for Joe, but there was still an air of doubt. Most of the evidence was circumstantial, and there was nothing concrete that factually linked Joe to the murder. There were a few who believed that Joe was innocent. Warden Allen himself was not totally convinced of Joe's guilt. At the time of Odette's murder, Joe was scheduled to appear before the parole board within a few weeks. It was said Mrs. Allen planned to speak to the parole board in his favor. Why would he ever harm Odette with his freedom so close and with her most likely being the key to that freedom?

Ida B. Wells, a famous activist, staunchly believed Joe was innocent and the victim of a political agenda. She read in Chicago papers that Joe had been in solitary in total darkness for fifty hours and had only been given bread and water to eat. She was outraged at the treatment Campbell received and sent her lawyer husband, Ferdinand Barnett, to his aid. Ida also personally visited Joe at the prison and came away from the meeting convinced of his innocence. Joe told her that his earlier confessions were coerced from him after exhaustion from having no food and undergoing constant interrogations. Despite their best efforts, Joe Campbell was found guilty of the murder of Odette Allen in November of 1915 and sentenced to be hanged. Ms. Wells continued to work tirelessly to raise money for Joe's cause while Ferdinand worked on getting the case to the Supreme Court. Joe was first set to be hanged on October 13, 1916. In a last-minute reprieve, the governor extended Joe's date a few months to December 8. Joe's life hung in the balance for almost two years while Barnett and his team worked to save him. Nothing the legal team did was working, but it did grant them some time.

The gallows had been moved from Cook County Jail to Old Joliet Penitentiary, where the hanging was to take place on Friday, April 12, 1918. On Thursday afternoon, April 11, only hours before Joe was to be hanged, the governor commuted his death sentence to life imprisonment. Joe lived out the rest of his life in Old Joliet Prison, and he eventually died in 1950. He proclaimed his innocence until the end.

After Odette's death, Warden Allen petitioned the governor to allow him to live outside the prison walls. He had sworn that he would never again step foot into the rooms where his wife had died. The governor denied Allen's request, citing the law that wardens must live on the premises as his reason. It was the last straw for Edmund Allen, and he resigned as warden of Joliet Penitentiary on August 7, 1915, leaving behind him not a legacy of honor, as he had hoped, but one of blood and tears. Warden Allen's departure was followed by the departure of Michael Zimmer. Warden Zimmer tried to continue what the Allens had started, but he only lasted two years. In that time, the prison went into a steady decline. Warden Zimmer's time

Current photograph of the entrance of Old Joliet Prison. The windows above the entrance look into the warden's quarters, and they are where images of dark shadow forms have been reported since the prison's closure. *Author's collection.*

with Joliet ended with violent rioting in 1917. Fire destroyed several of the prison's buildings, and the prison was obviously out of control.

A few days after the riots were snuffed out by the national guard, the governor appointed E.J. Murphy as the warden. Warden Murphy's appointment was the end of the era of leniency. He was given the position specifically because of his reputation of being a hard-core disciplinarian. Those who had always opposed the lenient ways of the Honor System blamed it for Odette's death. They had given trust to men who were not to be trusted. Two years later, chaos had done approximately $500,000 in damage. When incidents embarrass politicians and cost them loads of money, heads will roll. The riot halted prison reformists in their tracks for some time, and it was many years before modern changes would come again.

The remaining members of the Allen family who lived at the prison did not fare very well after Odette's death. Edmund Allen went on to eventually remarry one more time, and he spent the rest of his days living quietly in Chicago, working as a business promoter. He died of pneumonia in 1928 at the age of only fifty-three. Six years later, his son John died at thirty-eight years old due to complications from tuberculosis. Katherine lived to ninety years of age. Marrying and bearing six children, she surrounded herself with a large family who hopefully gave her comfort after the loss of so many loved ones.

The warden's quarters still sit quietly among the rooms in the administration building. Odette's bedroom is now spray-painted with graffiti, like most of the walls inside the Old Joliet Prison. Over the years, people have reported seeing shadows and dark figures in the windows of the administration building where Odette died as they passed by. Lights in the windows of the administration building were reported several times during the sixteen years the prison sat empty. In October of 2018, a photograph was taken in front of the prison before the very first nighttime tour. The photograph shows a white misty form that looks like a woman in a long white dress between the camera and the prison. Some believe that the captured figure, the shadows and the strange lights in the window could be beautiful Odette Allen roaming the prison grounds, patiently waiting and watching for her dress to arrive so that she can finally be reunited with Ned.

PART III

THE MAYHEM

Old Joliet Prison in the spring of 2020. *Author's collection.*

7
DEADLY ESCAPES

Escape attempts from Joliet numbered in the hundreds and ranged from comical attempts to deadly shootings. In the prison's earlier years, before modern forms of identification and communication, an inmate simply had to make it past the walls to freedom, where a couple of hops, skips and a name change could let them live their lives out undiscovered. The majority who made it out could not help but go back to their old haunts and habits, only to be captured and returned after a short stint of freedom. Some of the smarter escapees left Joliet behind to lead normal lives far away from the prison and its horrors. Some of these men went on to become successful, respected men in society, only to have their false identities exposed many years later. As successful as any of them became, the truth still surfaced. Most of these men were pardoned of their sentences, especially if they had come back on their own accord.

Getting over the wall and away from the immediate vicinity of the prison alive was the trick. Some would plot, plan and execute, successfully making it over the wall but not much farther. Escapees were treated with no mercy. Inmates attempting escape were shot on sight for many years. Sometimes, prisoners came up with clever and very comical ways to escape. Some were successful, but others were foiled by a simple mistake or just a bad stroke of luck.

Two convicts made their way to the prison hospital and proceeded to dress themselves as working nurses. They were able to walk right out of the prison undetected. In 1868, inmates used the help of a local shoemaker,

Razor wire at Old Joliet Prison in May 2014. *Author's collection.*

Firman Mack. Mr. Mack leased and operated the shoe shop inside the prison. One day, after hauling a load of finished shoes to his store, two prisoners burst out of one of the large boxes and ran away. Mr. Mack always checked his boxes from then on out. A short time later, another inmate attempted a similar stunt with a slight alteration. Instead of a shoe box, he removed a dead body from a coffin just before the funeral procession started. He placed himself inside and waited to be taken to the convict cemetery. As the coffin neared the cemetery, the prisoner inside became desperate for air. When he lifted the box just a bit for a small breath, he was discovered and returned to the prison. The same year, three inmates escaped with the help of an unknown individual outside the prison, who sawed the bars off the end of the sewer line.

One of the only attempts made by a woman was that of Mollie Brown. On visitation day, a male friend of Mollie's was able to slip a steel blade to her without anyone noticing. Mollie later caused trouble with the head matron on purpose so that she could be moved to a corner solitary cell on the fourth floor. The solitary cells in the women's prison were much better than those in the men's prison. The women's solitary cells contained small beds, complete with bedding and a window. With the steel blade, Mollie sawed through the window's bars and lowered herself down with a rope. Halfway down, the handmade rope broke. Mollie had mistakenly thought that the window of the cell opened above the roof of the adjacent cellhouse. It did not, and Mollie fell forty feet to the hard, stone-covered ground below. Mollie survived the fall but was permanently crippled.

Escape from the prison cells in the main prison was also a common problem in Joliet's earlier days. Prisoners would smuggle bread and small tools into their cells, and at night, while guards were not around, they would saw as much as they could through the bars undetected. Close to morning time, the convicts would mold the bread to the bars, concealing the dents they had made with a little help from some dirt for color. They would continue the process until the bars were nearly sawed through and able to be snapped off quickly. When the time was right, they would break through the last bit and attempt to make it outside the prison walls. With each escape attempt, the administration would learn and adjust prison protocols and rules to prevent further attempts. To solve the fake bread bar issue, guards would walk by each cell at the end of the night and bang on them with their night sticks. This would loosen and reveal any concealed damage to the cell doors.

David Pineda spent four years in the 1990s as an inmate in the east cellblock of Old Joliet Prison. On David's first night, he said he was just about to fall asleep on his cot when a strong vibration swept loudly through the rows of the east cellblock's iron bars, as if someone very large and powerful was banging on them. David could see no one alive or visible doing the banging when he looked to find the source of the vibrations. Was he hearing long-gone guards still checking the iron bars for saw marks?

Most escape attempts resulted in almost immediate capture, and as a result, escapees received punishments and additional time for their attempts. There were also those who came to deadly ends. Once, a prisoner who was assigned the job of waiter in the dining room decided he would squeeze himself under a sink after work, hoping to sneak out after hours to scale the wall and make his escape. A search commenced immediately when his absence was noticed, but no one could find the missing prisoner. Five days later, a horrible stench drew guards to the sink, and there, they found the convict dead. He had not been able to free himself and had suffocated.

A 1931 view from the restaurant across the street, where, that year, armed guards waited for prisoners who had reportedly escaped. *Courtesy of the Joliet Area Historical Museum.*

Current view of the southeast guard tower and Collins Street, where three escapees were shot and killed in 1931. *Author's collection.*

In 1931, the warden was informed of an escape plot that was being planned for February 22 that year. Just after midnight that day, three prisoners left the kitchen building, where they had been hiding, and made their way across the prison yard to the building in the southeast corner of the prison. They used the canopy over the entrance to climb on the roof and make their way to the prison wall. Unknown to the prisoners, guards armed with machine guns had been posted at a restaurant across the street from the prison and were waiting for them. As soon as the men were visible, the guards opened fire on the escaping prisoners. All three men were killed. The first was killed instantly on the roof of the building. The second and third were killed instantly as well. One fell from the roof and landed in the middle of Collins Street in front of the prison; the other landed at the bottom of the guard turret. The guards then pursued a car that had been ready and waiting for the escaped prisoners in a high-speed chase for miles. The car was finally able to outrun the police and was never captured.

The incident was later referred to by prisoners as Washington's Birthday Massacre, and it spurred a riot that was started at Old Joliet and continued days later at Stateville. The prisoners were outraged at the way the escape plot had been handled. Administration chose to station guards outside the prison who were ready to shoot and kill rather than station them inside the

Reverend George Whitmeyer, the prison chaplain and former convict who was accused of helping prisoners escape. *Courtesy of the Joliet Area Historical Museum.*

prison walls to intercept the escape attempt without anyone dying. In protest of the incident, Reverend George Whitmeyer, who had been serving as the prison's chaplain, resigned from his position. He publicly called the incident a senseless murder at the hands of the prison guards. After Whitmeyer's resignation, Warden Henry Hill told the press that he had intercepted the letters that the chaplain had carried outside the prison for convicts. An inmate had been brought to Warden Hill a few weeks before the chaplain resigned, and they had confessed that the holy man was riling inmates up by telling them that what the place needed was a good riot. The chaplain also was accused of having helped inmates by carrying out a story that was written by one of the prisoners. In the story was a secret code that detailed an upcoming escape plot. Whitmeyer later admitted that he had been a convict in New York before he became a reverend. He accused the prisons of gross misconduct and deplorable conditions.

In 2006, a woman who passed Old Joliet every night around 1:00 a.m. on her way home from work saw a strange man walking along the road next to the old prison. It was dark and very late, so the woman never even thought to stop but couldn't help but think it was very strange. A few seconds after she passed the man, curiosity made her look in her rearview mirror. There was no one there. The man she had just seen walking up the road had vanished.

She later recalled that she thought he was injured, as she noticed he was walking with a limp. She said that he looked very pale and was wearing what she described as something that looked like hospital scrubs (prison garb can sometimes look just like hospital garb). This account is reminiscent of the man who fell dead in the middle of the street in 1931. Did this woman see one of Joliet's famous haunts? Could the man have been the prisoner who was so brutally gunned down during his attempt to escape Old Joliet? Was he still searching for his getaway car? I would say this is all highly possible.

8

SUICIDES

Suicides were common occurrences in the old prison. On many levels, life inside Old Joliet was tough for most to deal with. The individuals serving life or long-term sentences were obviously not the stable types. Adding instability to a harsh environment was surely a recipe for disaster, as seen in the pages of this book. A life sentence inside Joliet was an ominous, black abyss of a future to stare into. Death, for some, was much easier than slowly wasting away.

Of the many suicides that happened on the grounds of Joliet Prison, none was more celebrated than that of Frank Rande. Rande made a name for himself for being one of the meanest men around. With a long history of petty crime and mischief as a boy, he grew to be a callous, aggressive man with no qualms about shooting anyone or anything that got in his way. In 1877, his criminal escapades across several states were sensational. He repeatedly escaped the clutches of the law, robbing stores and homes along his way. The newspapers kept readers in the area informed and aware. His crime sprees left a wake of destruction behind them. Wherever he went, someone turned up dead, even in prison.

Rande first served time for burglary in 1872 in his hometown in Iowa. He escaped one night but was captured a few days later and returned to the jail. Shortly after his return, another county picked him up to stand trial for charges against him in their district. During his transport by train, he pretended to be ill so that he could move to the back to vomit. He then jumped off the back of the train into a wooded culvert, escaping again. A few weeks later, he surfaced in Indianapolis, where he shot a police officer who was trying to arrest him. He ended up in Michigan City Penitentiary and was sentenced to five years for the murder of the officer. Rande left the Michigan prison after his release in 1877; he was more aggressive and hellbent on destruction than ever before. It was not long before he was up to no good. He started his legendary spree of bloodshed by relieving a local gunsmith of several guns and then continued a path of thievery and destruction all the way to St. Louis.

After he robbed a farmhouse in Gilson, Illinois, a group of neighboring farmers caught up with him in a wooded area. Trapped like the rat he was, Rande viciously turned on them and opened fire, leaving one dead and wounding several others. The small farming community was devastated. The public was outraged at the senseless tragedy and wanted Rande's head on a platter. He became one of the most wanted men in the country and was finally taken down in St. Louis, Missouri. Thirteen men were dead and several others left with severe injuries. For his crimes, Rande was sentenced to life in Joliet. Newspaper reporters described him as "one of the most unprincipled, bloodthirsty villains this country has ever seen." He arrived at the prison in February of 1878, still as full of fury as he ever was. Everywhere he went, he caused trouble or plotted an escape. Because of this, he was not only despised by the staff for being too difficult, but he was despised by his fellow prisoners as well.

Frank Rande was born an angry, aggressive individual, and he continued in this way every day of his life until the desperate end. An individual who grew up with Frank Rande wrote a letter to the editor of the *Ottumwa Daily Democrat* dated March of 1884. The writer knew Rande by his real name: Charlie Scott. In the letter, the writer told of his association with the Scott family as childhood neighbors. Charlie, also known as Frank, was one of the many sons of Matichi Scott, a well-to-do blacksmith in Fairfield, Iowa. The writer went on to say that the Scott boys were "tough cases" who were always looking for fights. Their father promoted the aggressive behavior and was said to excitedly leave his work behind to watch the fighting boys. Simply put, the Scott boys were all bullies, and if you messed with one, you ended up fighting them all.

Rande's stay in Joliet Penitentiary was chaotic to say the least. Many of his days were spent in solitary confinement as punishment for his transgressions inside the strict prison. Had Joliet not been the harsh place it was known to be, criminals like Rande would have easily roused other prisoners into trouble making. He was such a haunted individual that others sensed it as soon as he entered the room. He was pure evil.

At that time, the punishment for fighting and insubordination was as follows: the prisoner was taken to solitary confinement. For ten of the twenty-four hours in a day, they were shackled to the iron door of their cell. For the other fourteen hours, they could lay on a makeshift bed that consisted of a wooden board. A bucket was placed in the cell to be used as a toilet, and the only food they received was four ounces of bread and a pint of water per day. This pattern was repeated until the prisoner was too weak to stand. They were then transferred to the prison hospital, where they would recover and eventually be returned to the prison population. This punishment usually broke the hardest of men—but not Rande. He continued to be as rambunctious as ever, plotting his next escape as soon as he was back in population.

In March of 1884, Rande was working in one of the shops on the prison's grounds when he grabbed a fire poker and hit the deputy warden, McDonald, over the head. Two other inmates immediately tackled Rande to the ground and kept him there until Assistant Deputy Warden Garvin arrived. Garven then instructed them to take Rande to the deputy warden's office. On his way out, Rande made one last attempt to gain his freedom. A knife was lying on a worktable they passed as the guards led Rande toward the door; Rande managed to grab the knife and lunged at Garvin, slashing his arm. In the scuffle, Garvin managed to break his cane over Rande's head and then shoot him in the rib area. Simultaneously, McDonald managed to fire off a round that hit Rande in the head, finally rendering him unconscious. Incredibly, both bullets fired at Rande only skimmed him, leaving superficial wounds. He was examined by a doctor who determined he did not need further treatment, so he was immediately taken to solitary. This was the last time Rande was seen alive—or so the guards said.

The next morning, Rande was found dead, hanging from his cell door. He had used his prison uniform to form a noose and had launched himself from the waste bucket. An autopsy revealed that he had not broken his neck but had suffocated slowly. The story was that he had committed suicide because he was facing life in solitary. Some found it difficult to believe that this man, who was always so determined, in the end just gave up and went out quietly. It didn't seem like him at all, but there was no one around who really cared enough to make an issue of it.

The news that Frank Rande was finally dead spread like wildfire. Photographs were taken of his body hanging from the iron cell door. The population was relieved that this man was finally dead. Officials were more

Frank Rande's lifeless body after he hanged himself in the segregation cells. *Courtesy of the Joliet Area Historical Museum.*

than tired of his shenanigans before his last attempt in which he almost killed the deputy warden. The escape attempts always resulted in a panicked community, as someone always ended up dead. Everyone on the inside ultimately paid when rules were broken, especially the big ones related to escape and violence. Lockdowns, stricter rules and the withholding of the few privileges they had to look forward to were enough for Rande's fellow prisoners to turn against him as well. In the end, not even his family would claim him, and he was buried in the old Joliet convict cemetery that was less than a mile from the old prison.

Rande's life and death were so sensational that the prison was offered $1,000 for his body and the prison door he hanged himself on for a museum display. The offer was denied. The photograph of Frank Rande's lifeless body on the cell door is one of the most popular to surface when researching the old prison. His story still lives on in the retelling of his escapades during tours. One must wonder if Frank is still hanging around Old Joliet, listening in on and regaling in the retellings of his glory days as an outlaw and general badass.

James Pangburn only spent seven days in Old Joliet before he took his own life. The only note he left behind was found inside his stomach during his autopsy. Pangburn was convicted of burglary and given a sentence of thirty months of probation in 1979. He violated his probation twice. The first violation was for possession of marijuana, and he served ninety days on work release in a county jail. The second violation came when he was caught trying to steal tools; for this, he was sentenced to one year in Old Joliet. Within his first few days, he was moved to a protective custody cell (solitary) after it was reported he was sexually assaulted and that someone was planning to shank, or stab, him.

One week after his arrival for petty crimes, twenty-one-year-old James Pangburn was found hanging in his cell. The autopsy the next day revealed that James had written and swallowed two small notes just before his death. One said, "Disciples had keys to door." And the other said, "The police killed me." The Disciples were a ruling gang inside Joliet at the time. Two days after his death, Pangburn's fiancée received a letter from him that he had written the day he died. In the letter, James had begged her to call the warden of the prison to let him know that his life was in danger. He said there was a contract on his head and that the guards had been paid off and did not care. His mother told reporters that when she had talked to him last, he had been very scared. This was apparent, as it was reported to have taken the guards fifteen minutes to get into his cell the morning of his death. Pangburn had torn his bedsheets into strips of cloth and woven them into intricate knots all around his cell door. The man was obviously terrified to the point of insanity. The Pangburn family believed that James had been murdered and filed a $25 million lawsuit against the Illinois Department of Corrections. James Pangburn's death was never officially ruled a suicide or homicide by Will County coroners. It is unknown at this point what happened with the lawsuit. Surely, it was settled out of court and privately.

Suicides were not just prevalent on the inside, but they were prevalent among people who worked for the prison. Several accounts have been located from employees of the prison, both onsite staff and those who worked within the administration, who had committed suicide. Was it the prison environment they worked in that caused such utter despair that they decided they could no longer bear it, or was it something else altogether reaching its icy fingers out to grasp the vulnerable? In the latter half of 1894, three officials linked to the Joliet prison committed suicide within five weeks of each other.

The first of these workers was Gallus Mueller, who had been the chief clerk at Joliet Prison for over twenty years when he committed suicide by shooting himself through the heart on November 1, 1894. He was most famously known for introducing the Bertillon System to the United States, which consisted of documenting measurements, physical descriptions and other characteristics to identify prisoners. Joliet was one of the first prisons in the country to use this method. Other penal institutions across the country promptly followed Joliet's shining example in adopting the method. Mueller's suicide stunned everyone. He was well-respected and liked throughout the country. Highly educated, he was said to have spoken several different languages fluently. He seemed to be a reasonably happy man with a family and successful career. Still, something distressed him enough that he felt taking his life was the better option. There was no note left to explain, and there was never an answer as to why he committed suicide.

Just over a month later, Robert Huston, a former sheriff of Will County, was found dead in his room at the Grand Pacific Hotel in Chicago. An empty vial that had contained the poison he had taken was found next to him on the bed. He, too, was well known and respected throughout the city. After his death, it was made public that he had lost $4,000 through the Chicago Trade Board during his term as sheriff (the equivalent of that in today's money is approximately $120,000). The newspaper reported that he was soon facing large bills with no way to pay them, so he opted to take his life instead of facing the embarrassment of what was coming.

Captain James S. Miller was the third. He had been the head engineer at Joliet Prison for twenty-two years when he was forced into retirement during an administration change. Shortly after his retirement, and only seven days after Huston was found dead, James Miller shot himself at his home. He also seemed to have been a reasonably happy individual. He left behind him a considerable estate, a wife and five grown children. He had reached seventy-six years of age and was comfortable, surrounded by family and financially set. Still, something was horrible enough to distress this man so badly that he could bear it no longer. Again, there was no note and no explanation.

With all three suicides happening within weeks of each other, it is hard not to wonder if there was a connection. Was this string of suicides just a mere coincidence or was there something more to it? Two of the three men spent good portions of their lives inside the limestone walls of Old Joliet. They were all exposed to the hard, brutal life that the prisoners led. Was it just too much sorrow for them to bear, or did something slowly seep inside them from all those years of being in such a dark place of death and destruction?

9

EXECUTIONS

T he death penalty was officially abolished in Illinois on March 9, 2011, by Governor Pat Quinn. Those on death row at the time of the change had their sentences converted to life in prison. Execution by hanging was the form of capital punishment used in Illinois until 1928, when the electric chair was introduced. The chair was used until 1962. No more executions occurred for the next ten years. In 1972, the Supreme Court handed down a ruling that banished the death penalty in all states. In 1973, Illinois legislature passed a bill for the death penalty to be reinstated. The law took effect as of July 1, 1973, but was struck down by the Supreme Court in 1972. In June of 1977, the death penalty was reinstated by Illinois and was held up by the Supreme Court in 1977; it stayed that way until 2011, when the death penalty was abolished in Illinois once again.

Throughout all the back and forth, the next execution did not happen until 1990. By then, lethal injection was deemed the more humane method of execution and was used from then on. Electric chairs were still housed in some of the state prisons across the country as an option if lethal injection was not possible or if it was requested by the inmate.

Three locations in Illinois held executions: Joliet, Cook County and Menard. Joliet's territory was everything north of Springfield and Menard's was everything south of Springfield. The exception was Cook County, which had its own domain. A total of twelve documented executions took place on the grounds of Old Joliet Prison. The first time the electric chair was used in

Old Joliet was on December 15, 1928. It was also the first time "Old Sparky" was used in Illinois. In grand Old Joliet style, not only one man, but three men were put to death that day. Dominic Bressetti, Claude Clark and John Brown had been convicted of burglary and murder. In May of that year, they had broken into and robbed a farmhouse. During the robbery, they killed the farmer and brutally beat the farmer's wife. All three were tried and given the death sentence. The three executions were completed one after the other on the same date. It only took a total of seventeen minutes for each man to sit in the chair and be declared dead.

The next execution at the prison did not happen for several years, but it was also a triple execution. Four Rockford men had robbed the Lenore, Illinois State Bank, killing cashier J. Charles Bundy and two police officers in the high-speed chase afterward. Police had cornered Melvin Fleist in a cornfield in Varna, Illinois, when he turned his gun on himself and committed suicide. The remaining three bandits, Arthur Thielen (forty-two), Fred Garner (twenty-seven, Thielen's brother-in-law) and John Hauff (thirty-two), were holed up by police in a farmhouse nearby.

In December of 1937, John Jelliga and Michael Munjas showed up at the farm of Mr. and Mrs. Edward Pansa in Crete, Illinois. The men had come to the Pansa home believing that the couple had $2,000 in cash from a recent inheritance. When the couple denied any such money, Mr. Pansa was struck with the butt of a gun and dragged into another room. His wife heard the men quarrel violently with her husband, and then she heard a gunshot accompanied by her husband's piercing scream. She then heard the men ransack her home before they came back to confront her again. They told her that they had to shoot her husband because he had recognized them, and they said they were going to kill her too. They then shot Mrs. Pansa, point blank, in the head and left, thinking she was dead. Mrs. Pansa, although severely wounded, was still alive. After the men left, she dragged herself, on all fours, for three-quarters of a mile in the snow to her brother's farm. Mrs. Pansa did not only recover but went on to identify both Jelliga and Munjas.

After being arrested in their homes, both men would confess to having killed Edward, tortured Mrs. Pansa and stolen seventy-seven dollars in cash. Neither of the men had ever been arrested before. Munjas committed suicide in the Will County Jail while awaiting trial; Jelliga was given the death penalty. The day before he was scheduled to be executed, Jelliga sat on death row, while nearby, Warden Ragen did several tests with the electric chair. The loud electric hum seemed to overtake the entire facility.

The southeast guard tower. *Author's collection.*

The prison band tried to drown out the sound by playing music loudly. At 12:03 a.m. on December 21, 1938, John Jelliga was executed via the electric chair in Old Joliet with more than forty people in attendance. Jelliga was buried in the Illinois State Prison Cemetery on the prison's property. He left behind a wife and two small children.

The last execution in Illinois occurred in 1999.

PART IV

STATEVILLE

10

STATEVILLE PRISON

Time eventually caught up with the Old Joliet Prison. By the early 1900s, the need for a new facility became necessary once again. Calls for closure had begun as early as 1877, with officials claiming it was already outdated and overcrowded. In 1907, 2,200 acres of land was purchased five miles northwest of Old Joliet for a new state prison. Construction began in 1916, with a temporary wooden stockade built around the 64 acres that would eventually be the Stateville Prison. As with the old prison, the early construction at Stateville was done mainly by convict labor.

Before construction began on the main facility, a three-person committee was sent to Europe to study prison designs. They particularly liked the ideas of philosopher Jeremy Bentham, who thought panopticon (all-seeing) cellhouses was optimal for prisons. The cells would be built in a circular shape, with a tower in the middle of the building so that guards could have a 360-degree view of the entire building. The first of the four circular buildings was completed in 1919. The original plans called for eight round buildings that would surround a round dining room in a wagon wheel–type design. Above-ground tunnels running from each cellhouse to the dining hall would enable easy and secure transport of inmates to meals. Only three more of the round buildings were built; the last was finished in 1927. Plans for the remaining four were scrapped, and the next cellhouse wasn't built until 1931. It was a large rectangular building known as Cellhouse B. The building was 444 feet long and 56 feet wide with 580 cells inside. That same year, the four-story administration building was finished.

The Stateville location carried on Old Joliet's reputation for mayhem and death. In December 1921, during construction inside one of the round buildings, a scaffolding structure that was holding five workers collapsed and fell fifty feet. One man was killed and the four others seriously injured. The jail was only officially open for a year before its first murder. In May of 1926, seven inmates, all of whom were convicted murderers, escaped after killing Deputy Warden Peter Klein. The seven inmates, Robert Torrez, Charles Duchowski, Walter Stalsky, James Price, Charles Shader, Bernardo Roa and Gregorio Rizzo, were admitted to the deputy warden's office for a regular meeting about prison conditions. When they were alone with Klein, the men brutally attacked him, stabbing him repeatedly. They then took four of the five other employees who had been in the office to solitary cells and locked them in. The fifth prison employee who had been in the office that morning was Captain J.W. Keely. The gang of escapees took Keely to the front gates of the prison, where they forced him to call for a car. Thinking that Keely was calling for the deputy warden, they sent Klein's personal vehicle. They then kidnapped a trustee named Cassidy to drive the car out of the prison. The seven drove away from the prison with Cassidy and Keely in tow.

No one discovered what had happened until after the escapees were well away from the prison. Immediately, armed guards were sent out in cars on all the roads leading from the prison. Once word reached the neighboring communities, locals joined the search and formed a massive manhunt. Once they were a good distance from the prion, the fugitives stopped the car and handcuffed the two kidnapped men to a tree. After ditching the hostages, the seven inmates split into two groups. Two of the men took off on foot, and the remaining five ditched the car about an hour southwest of the prison, in Sandy Ford Valley, before walking a short distance to the closest town, Lenore. While walking, they looted farmhouses on the outskirts of town, arming themselves with guns they found on the way. When they reached the town line, they encountered a posse of twenty policemen and local men waiting for them. A massive shootout ensued, with hundreds of bullets flying. In the end, two inmates were captured, and two police officers were wounded. Eventually, six of the original seven were captured. James Price was the only one who got away.

The six who were captured were convicted of murder and sentenced to hang on the same day in February of 1927. A stay was granted, pending an appeal to the Supreme Court. While awaiting the appeal, Torrez, Roa and Rizzo managed to escape from the Will County Jail, where they were being held. All three made it to Chicago, where police caught up with them.

Another deadly shootout occurred, resulting in the death of an officer and the capture of Torrez and Rizzo. Roa escaped recapture and was rumored to be hiding in Mexico. Two days before they were to be hanged, Shader, Duchowski, Rizzo and Stalsky tried to escape yet again. During this attempt, Rizzo was killed, and Shader escaped. Duchowski and Stalsky were recaptured and hanged two days later, along with Torrez, on July 15, 1927, at the Will County Jail in Illinois's first triple execution. Shader was captured in June of 1928 and was hanged in October that year. Bernardo Roa and James Price were never captured.

In 1931, a riot broke out at the Old Joliet Prison that carried over to Stateville four days later. Trouble had been brewing with inmates due to recent events, like the Washington Birthday Massacre (detailed in Chapter 1), in which three inmates who were trying to escape were ruthlessly gunned down in the street. The riot caused $500,000 worth of damage to several prison buildings.

In 1935, Joseph Ragen took the position of warden of both prisons and immediately cleaned them up. After clearing the prison yards, where prisoners had handmade wood shanties and were openly engaging in illegal activities, Ragen put the inmates to work. He leveled the prison yard by making prisoners hand carry dirt from one place to another. After the ground was level, the prison yard was slowly transformed into beautiful green lawns and flower gardens. About 550,000 flowers were grown in the prison's greenhouses and planted around the property. The landscaping was so stunning that it won garden club awards, and visitors would come from miles around to see the gardens.

Richard Loeb, one half of the murdering duo who killed young Bobby Franks in 1924, was in an altercation with another inmate at Stateville Prison, who slashed him over fifty times with a straight razor. Loeb died in the prison hospital shortly after the incident.

In 1937, Warden Ragen established a new cemetery close to the Stateville location: the Illinois State Prison (ISP) Cemetery. It took the place of the older convict cemetery near the Old Joliet Prison. Inmates who died on prison property and were unclaimed afterward were buried in ISP after its establishment. The headstones in ISP were made in the prison's terra-cotta shop and were etched simply with a name and number. A large dedication stone sits in the middle of the open field in which the old cemetery sits. It reads, "They Paid Their Debt to Society, May God Remit Their Debt to Him." From 1925 to 1974, 436 male inmates and 1 female inmate were buried in the ISP Cemetery that sits a bit closer to Stateville's wall. In the early 1970s, new laws were instated that said all inmate deaths on prison grounds required an autopsy. Since the county had to pick up the body anyway, they took care of burial arrangements. Right around the time that these laws went into effect, burials on prison grounds were stopped.

Three of the thirteen inmates executed in Joliet prisons were buried in ISP. John Brown, one of the men executed in Illinois's first use of the electric chair, was buried here. John was one of three men to be electrocuted in the chair that day in 1928. It took only seventeen minutes to carry out all of the electrocutions and pronounce all three dead. John Jelliga, who was also executed in the chair in Old Joliet, was buried in ISP. A longtime caretaker of the prison grounds said that Jelliga's family was one of the only families to bury a prisoner in this cemetery with a personal service and flowers. In addition to inmates' unclaimed bodies, six human limbs were buried in the cemetery. Through the years, some inmates required the amputation of a limb at the prison hospital. The prison had to show proof of how the limb was disposed of, so four legs, one arm and one hand are buried between other intact graves.

Stateville was plagued by escape attempts, just as every prison usually is. Some, like Henry J. Fernekes, chose the permanent escape route: suicide. Fernekes stood only five feet four inches tall; his tiny stature and vicious nature earned him the name Midget Killer. Fernekes's criminal career included multiple robberies, three murdered men and a long list of other violent crimes. He was sent to Old Joliet in 1925 on a one-year-to-life sentence. In August of 1935, a female visitor managed to smuggle a set of civilian clothes to Fernekes. After changing into them unseen, he walked right out of the prison, undetected. Guards were baffled for a good while as to how he had escaped. After twelve weeks of "French leave," Fernekes was captured and returned. This time, he was moved to the more secure Stateville facility. His stealth was proven once again shortly after his return to prison. Somehow, despite two thorough searches, Fernekes managed to smuggle a vial of poison into his cell. Guards found him dead in his cell the next morning. Fernekes's escape amazed prison administration, but it also called for the need to regulate prison visitors. From then on, all visitors were required to sign in and out of the prison.

Warden Ragen resigned from his position in March 1941, after a new governor was elected. He was afraid that political influence would interfere with his work at the prison. His resignation only lasted nineteen months. In October of 1942, infamous Roger "The Terrible" Touhy and six other inmates escaped. Within days of the escape, Warden Ragen was reinstated, with promises that nothing political would interfere with his administration at Stateville. After a few months, two of the escapees were gunned down, and the other five were captured.

During World War II, 480 convicts at Stateville voluntarily participated in a malaria research project at the prison. Malaria-carrying mosquitos were raised on prison grounds and then were used to bite the volunteer inmates. The volunteers who contracted the disease were supervised by doctors who were trying to find a cure. Soldiers fighting in the South Pacific made finding a cure urgent. During the experiment, several new drugs were discovered that revolutionized the treatment of the horrible disease. Nathan Leopold, the other half of the duo who murdered Bobby Franks in 1924, was one of the 480 inmates who participated in the malaria study. Many of the inmates who participated were never promised any rewards for their participation, but they did receive some time off their sentences. Warden Ragen saw the prisons through their best days, until he permanently resigned in 1962.

In 1995, an anonymous tip came in saying that a man had been murdered at Stateville and buried on property. After searching the area where the body was reported to have been buried, officials found a human skull in one of the prison yards. Through dental records, the skull was confirmed to belong to Carlos Robles. Robles went missing from Stateville in 1983, only one week before he was due to be released. The rest of Robles's body was never found, and no other mention of the incident was made.

Richard Speck spent twenty-four years in Stateville Prison for brutally stabbing and strangling eight student nurses in Chicago in 1966. One survivor identified Speck as the killer in part by the "Born to Raise Hell" tattoo he had permanently inked on his arm. Speck was convicted and originally given the death sentence, but the sentence was commuted to 50 to 150 years for each murder. In 1983, Speck happily told reporters that he loved Stateville and that it was his home. In his earlier years there, he was a troublemaker but mellowed with age. He worked on a wall-painting crew in the prison and occasionally did oil paintings of his own. One of the more infamous stories associated with Speck was re-created in a scene on the recent series *Mindhunter*. On the show, two FBI agents interview Speck at Stateville. When Speck enters the room, he has a small bird in his hands. He tells the agents that he found the bird injured in the prison yard and had nursed him back to health. They are surprised at the tenderness he shows the animal, but the feeling is short-lived. When the interview is finished, Speck is told by a guard that he is not allowed to take the bird with him and that he must let him go. In a rage, Speck throws the bird into a large fan above, smashing the poor animal to pieces. The guard and agents are stunned, and Speck says, "If I can't have him, nobody can." The incident is said to have happened, although not during an FBI interview. Richard Speck died at Stateville in 1993, one day shy of his fiftieth birthday.

The most famous man to visit Stateville was John Wayne Gacy. In 1979, police found thirty-three bodies buried in various states of decomposition in the crawl space of Gacy's home in Norridge, Illinois. He spent twenty-one hours in the Old Joliet Prison before being processed out to spend most of his sentence at Menard, where he sat on death row for twelve years. Gacy returned to Stateville in 1994—it was his last trip. John Wayne Gacy was put to death by lethal injection on May 10, 1994, at Stateville Prison in Joliet, Illinois. As a crowd of thousands gathered outside Stateville's wall, chanting and calling for his demise, Gacy uttered his last words, "Kiss my ass."

PART V

TOURS AND RESTORATION

The Old Joliet Prison closed its doors for good in 2002. It stood empty for sixteen years; during that time, its fate was uncertain. There were those who believed the prison should be restored and used for tourism due to its historical significance. The obstacle to this was always how to achieve the very large goal of restoring the prison to a working independent historical tour site. In 2018, the Joliet Area Historical Museum began giving tours of the old prison to raise money for the restoration. They continue to work slowly toward their goal, and today, you can tour the old jail from spring until fall through the museum. In the summer of 2020, they began offering public and private paranormal investigations. Proceeds from all tours and events go toward restoration efforts.

Old Joliet Prison's entrance. *Author's collection.*

It will take thousands of dollars and man hours to achieve the goal of restoring the penitentiary to an independent historical tour site. All types of volunteering and donating play big parts in rescuing this institution. Time and money are always the top needs in this type of project. If you would like to help the restoration effort or if you are interested in taking a tour or holding an event at Old Joliet Prison, please visit the Joliet Area Historical Museum website for more information:

www.jolietmuseum.org

BIBLIOGRAPHY

News Articles

Alton Evening Telegraph. "Rebel Joliet Radio Band Disciplined." March 25, 1936.

Babwin, Don. "Forgotten in Death." *Chicago Tribune*, August 24, 1997.

Billings Gazette Sun. "Illinois Burns Three Killers for Killing Man." December 16, 1928.

Bookwalter, Genevieve. "Outside Chicago, Historic Old Joliet Prison Is Open for Tours—At Least for Now." *Washington Post*, April 12, 2019.

———. "Where's Jake's Cell? At Old Joliet Prison, That's the Big Question." *Philadelphia Inquirer*, December 20, 2019.

Boone News Republic. "Death in Joliet Prison." December 1, 1921.

Carlozob, Lou. "Prison Blues." *Chicago Tribune*, February 18, 2002.

Dolan Weekly Eagle. "Five Recaptured, One Still at Large." March 18, 1927.

Evening Tribune. "Convicted Man Fears Death in Joliet Prison." January 16, 1930.

Gallagher, Harry S. "Whiting Man Will Die for Crete Murder." *Hammond Times*, October 20, 1938.

Khazan, Olga. "Nearly Half of All Murdered Women Are Killed by Romantic Partners." *Atlantic*, n.d.

Lawrence Daily Journal. "The Joliet Executions." January 19, 1894.

Steubenville Herald Star. "Loeb Slashed by Convict." January 28, 1936.

Swancer, Bret. "Ghosts and the Weird World of the Stone Tape Theory." Mysterious Universe. www.mysteriousuniverse.org.

Wilmington Independent, October 18, 1865.

Websites

Ancestry. www.ancestry.com.

Blanco, Juan. Murderpedia. www.murderpedia.org.

Find a Grave. www.findagrave.com.

Gregory, Terry. Chicagology. www.chicagology.com.

Illinois Genealogy Trails History Group. "Transcriptions of the Joliet, Illinois Prison Convict Registers." www.genealogytrails.com.

IMDb. www.imdb.com.

Loerzel, Robert. Alchemy of Bones. www.alchemyofbones.com.

Movie Maps. "Movies Filmed at Joliet Prison." www.moviemaps.org.

Taylor, Troy. American Hauntings. www.americanhauntingsink.com.

Other Publications

Bowen, A.L. "Joliet Prison and the Riots of June 5th." *Journal of Criminal Law and Criminology* 8, no. 4 (1918).

Whiteside, John. "The History of Joliet." *Herald News*, 2001.

Books

Clearfield, Dylan. *Chicagoland Ghosts*. San Diego, CA: Thunder Bay Press, 1997.

Erickson, Gladys A. *Warden Ragen of Joliet*. New York: Dutton, 1957.

Lindberg, Richard. *Return to the Scene of the CRIME*. Nashville, TN: Cumberland House Publishing, 1999.

Sterling, Robert E. *Joliet Prisons: Images in Time*. St. Louis, MO: G. Bradley Publishing Inc., 2003.

About the Author

Author Wendy Moxley Roe in Bachelor's Grove Cemetery in Midlothian, Illinois. *Author's collection.*

Wendy Moxley Roe originally moved to the Chicago area from south central Pennsylvania in 2008. A photographer, history buff, cemetery enthusiast and paranormal investigator, Wendy is best known for her work with Bachelor's Grove Cemetery in Midlothian, Illinois. With her research partner, Karl K., Wendy designed and built the Path to Bachelor's Grove, which the pair continues to maintain. The Path to Bachelor's Grove includes a website, traveling exhibit and multiple social media sites dedicated to Bachelor's Grove Cemetery. Information and photographs from the Path to Bachelor's Grove were also featured in The History Press's 2016 book *Haunted Bachelor's Grove Cemetery*.

Wendy went to Old Joliet Prison for the first time in the spring of 2014. That visit started Wendy's five-year exploration into the research that appears in *Haunted Joliet Prison*. In 2019, Wendy launched *Tombstone Travels*, a blog that collects the cemetery-related, historical and paranormal stories she was writing at the time. The blog became the catalyst for *Haunted Joliet Prison*. Wendy currently lives in the Chicago suburbs with her cat, Jax.